INSPIRE / PLAN / DISCOVER / EXPERIENCE

WASHINGTON, DC

CONTENTS

DISCOVER 6

EXPERIENCE 48

NEED TO KNOW 190

Left: The Rotunda at the United States Capitol
Previous page: The Washington Monument seen from the Lincoln Memorial
Front cover: Sunrise reflected in the Lincoln Memorial pool

DISCOVER

Bird's-eye view of the Lincoln Memorial

WELCOME TO
WASHINGTON, DC

Museums filled with wonders. Galleries bursting with masterworks. Lush, verdant parks and gardens. And everywhere famous views that every visitor knows by heart. This is a city in renaissance, a grand dream of marble and art, of substance and spectacle. Wherever you turn, there are marvels to be discovered, and discoveries that defy description. Whatever your dream trip to Washington, DC entails, this DK Eyewitness Travel Guide is the perfect companion.

1 The Potomac in Mather Gorge, Great Falls.

2 Fala the dog, Franklin D. Roosevelt Memorial.

3 Aircraft at the National Air and Space Museum.

4 The Jefferson Memorial at the Tidal Basin.

Washington, DC is undergoing a miraculous metamorphosis as whole neighborhoods are rebuilt and reborn. The city has rediscovered its waterfront in a big way, building gardens, parks, and bike paths along the Potomac River, and creating fabulous waterfront developments like National Harbor and District Wharf.

The heart of the city is the Mall, ringed with famous museums and grand monuments. Renowned airplanes and spacecraft inspire the dreams of tomorrow at the National Air and Space Museum, while science comes to life among the diamonds and dinosaurs of the National Museum of Natural History. The stately Northwest district is home to the grand mansions of Embassy Row, the magnificent Washington National Cathedral, and the must-see National Zoo. Historic Georgetown offers chic shopping and a gourmand's delight of dining options. The Capitol Hill and Penn Quarter neighborhoods offer more fine dining and unique attractions such as the National Archives and the US Botanic Garden.

Washington is a small gem, but so packed with attractions, so full of things to see and do, that it can be hard to know where to start. We've broken the city down into easily navigable chapters, with detailed itineraries, expert local knowledge, and colorful, comprehensive maps to help you plan the perfect visit. Whether you're staying for a weekend, a week, or longer, this Eyewitness guide will ensure that you see the very best America's capital has to offer. Enjoy the book, and enjoy Washington, DC.

REASONS TO LOVE
WASHINGTON, DC

Small but deliciously beautiful, Washington, DC delights at every turn. Any list of its treasures must include its famed museums, magnificent memorials, green spaces, and secret sanctuaries. Here are a few of our favorites.

1 THE MALL

Often called "America's front yard," the Mall (p62) is an amazing collection of museums, gardens, and beautiful memorials that are the centerpiece of America's capital.

AMAZING ARCHITECTURE 2

The city's architects want you to know that this is an important city, and they do it with architectural eye candy, from the Neo-Classical Supreme Court (p56) to the Beaux Arts Union Station (p59).

3 TIDAL BASIN

An unexpected treat on the west end of the Mall is this scenic pool (p85), edged by a walking path that offers postcard views and shaded places to sit beneath the cherry trees.

NATIONAL GALLERY OF ART 4

One of the world's greatest collections, the gallery *(p66)* has works ranging from antiquities to pop art, including *Multiverse*, this striking light sculpture by Leo Villareal.

UNITED STATES CAPITOL 5

Every country has one overwhelmingly iconic building, and in America it is the spectacularly domed Capitol *(p54)*, which has become a symbol of the nation's political strength.

LINCOLN MEMORIAL 6

As well as a memorial to the most revered US president, this somber statue *(p84)* is a touchstone for the Civil Rights movement and a symbol of social justice. The upper steps offer the best view of the Mall anywhere.

CHERRY BLOSSOMS 7
Few things can compare to walking beneath cherry trees whose branches support floating clouds of delicate blossoms. Originally a gift from Japan, thousands of cherry trees now stand in the Mall area *(p62).*

THE RIVERFRONT 8
The Potomac *(p26)* has become a symbol of the city's renaissance. Cycling and walking paths and lush parks line the river's edge, and its waters teem with boaters.

9 DISTRICT WHARF
This multi-billion-dollar development *(p136)* offers riverfront dining, marinas, and shopping and concerts by the water. The Wharf jitney is the cheapest cruise in DC (it's free!).

10 GEORGETOWN

Georgetown *(p118)* is blue jeans and martinis, sophistication and coolness. Relax on a sunny afternoon at the waterfront park, or people-watch at Dean & DeLuca.

A SEAT IN THE GALLERIES 11

One of the great things about Washington is that you can witness the government in action. Watch Supreme Court *(p56)* arguments or bills being passed in the Capitol *(p54)*.

MARVELOUS MUSEUMS 12

It would take weeks to see all of Washington's famed museums, which boast spectacular exhibits such as Barbara Kruger's text-based installation *Belief +Doubt* at the Hirshhorn.

National Zoo

WOODLEY PARK

GLOVER PARK

Rock Creek Park

Meridian Hill Park

Whitehaven Park

KALORAMA

ADAMS-MORGAN

Dumbarton Oaks

NORTHWEST
p146

Oak Hill Cemetery

Dupont Circle

Scott Circle

Georgetown University

GEORGETOWN
p118

National Geographic Museum

Chesapeake and Ohio Canal

Washington Circle

Washington Harbour

FOGGY BOTTOM

Lafayette Square

NORTH HIGHLAND

Roosevelt Island

Georgetown Channel

WHITE HOUSE AND FOGGY BOTTOM
p104

White House

Little River

ROSSLYN

National Museum of African American History and Culture

Lincoln Memorial

THE MALL
p62

Washington Monument

Arlington National Cemetery

Lady Bird Johnson Park

United States Holocaust Memorial Museum

Potomac River

Tidal Basin

EXPLORE
WASHINGTON, DC

This guide divides Washington, DC into seven color-coded sightseeing areas, as shown on the map above. Find out more about each area on the following pages. For sights beyond the city center see p158, and for day trips out of Washington, DC see p174.

NORTH AMERICA

CANADA

• Seattle

U S A

Chicago • • Boston
San Francisco • • New York
WASHINGTON, DC •

• Los Angeles
Memphis • *Atlantic Ocean*

• Atlanta

Houston •
Gulf of Mexico • Miami

MEXICO

Pacific Ocean

COLUMBIA HEIGHTS

CARDOZO-SHAW

Howard University

African American Civil War Museum

Logan Circle

Gallaudet University

Mt Vernon Square

SAAM and NPG

PENN QUARTER
p88

Columbus Circle

National Archives

Newseum

CAPITOL HILL
p50

Stanton Square

National Museum of Natural History

National Gallery of Art

US Capitol

Lincoln Park

National Air and Space Museum

Seward Square

Museum of the Bible

International Spy Museum

SOUTH OF THE MALL
p132

Washington Channel

District Wharf

WATERFRONT

East Potomac Park

Nationals Park

Navy Yard Park

Navy Museum

ANACOSTIA

Anacostia River

| 0 kilometers | | 1 |
| 0 miles | | 0.5 |

N
↑

GETTING TO KNOW
WASHINGTON, DC

America's capital is the seat of government. It is also a massively popular destination, with tens of millions of visitors each year. For those ready to explore beyond museums and monuments, there is a colorful collection of distinctive neighborhoods, each with its own personality and pulse.

PAGE 50

CAPITOL HILL

The Capitol may be the most iconic image of American democracy in the world. A tour of the building, with its ornate architecture, remarkable artworks, and world-shaping history, is a great place to start. An easy walk away lie the exquisite Union Station, the historic shops of Eastern Market, and block after block of elegant row houses.

Best for
Watching the governing of the United States

Home to
United States Capitol

Experience
A tour of the grand Capitol building and lunch at Eastern Market

PAGE 62

THE MALL

The place everyone wants to see, but no one can see it all – there's just too much! The Mall is a glorious 2-mile- (3.5-km-) long swath of emerald lawn, dotted by park-like spaces and gardens. It is bordered on the eastern half by some of the world's most famous museums and on the western half by grand and powerful memorials to the nation's leaders and history.

Best for
Monuments and museums

Home to
National Air and Space Museum, National Museum of African American History and Culture

Experience
The view across the Mall from the steps of the Lincoln Memorial

PENN QUARTER

Penn Quarter is business-casual. Home to famous non-profits, lobby groups, and think tanks, this neighborhood also offers fine restaurants, lesser-known memorials, and a handful of truly wonderful, if quirky, museums. The area is also home to several food and wine festivals and a popular weekly farmers market outside the Smithsonian American Art Museum (SAAM).

Best for
Fascinating, lesser-known museums

Home to
Newseum, SAAM and NPG

Experience
The fabulous view of the United States Capitol building and Pennsylvania Avenue from the Newseum's Greenspun Terrace, and a glimpse of the historic, original US Constitution at the National Archives

WHITE HOUSE AND FOGGY BOTTOM

The grand centerpiece of this area is the Executive Mansion, also known as the White House. If you have not arranged for a tour in advance, you can still enjoy the iconic views of the mansion from the north and south sides. Lafayette Square offers great people-watching and is surrounded by historic homes and buildings. Also in this area are the renowned Renwick Gallery and the Kennedy Center.

Best for
Strolling through Lafayette Park, enjoying the famous views of the White House and watching the ever-present protesters, bustling news crews, and throngs of tourists from around the world

Home to
The White House

Experience
A tour of the White House (reserve before your trip), and a performance at the Kennedy Center

→

GEORGETOWN

Elegant and cool, Georgetown is a hub of education, history, culture, and outdoor activities all rolled into one. Its historic row houses have seen a who's who of residents, from Thomas Jefferson to the Kennedys. Nature beckons in the stunning gardens of Dumbarton Oaks and along the lovely Chesapeake and Ohio Canal. This is also DC's trendiest shopping and dining area.

Best for
Shopping, dining, enjoying the outdoors

Home to
Chesapeake and Ohio Canal, Dumbarton Oaks

Experience
A paddle on the Potomac (rent a kayak at Thompson Boat House), and shopping at the one-of-a-kind Sunday Georgetown Flea Market

SOUTH OF THE MALL

District Wharf (or locally just "the Wharf") is a glittering mini-city. This is where the river lives. Four piers, two marinas, and two parks offer boat tours, live riverfront music, a thriving seafood market, water taxis, and lots of places to watch the river roll by.

Best for
Waterfront dining and strolling

Home to
United States Holocaust Memorial Museum

Experience
Fresh steamed seafood at Captain White's, and a water taxi ride – a fun, cheap cruise

NORTHWEST

The western part of Northwest is full of 100-year-old mansions built by the wealthy and powerful; to the east, the largely African-American neighborhoods of U Street and Shaw were once known as the "Black Broadway." Today, this is one of the city's hippest areas.

Best for
Great architecture, lively music and entertainment

Home to
Embassy Row

Experience
Renoir's Afternoon of the Boating Party at the Phillips Gallery, followed by dinner and a show at the Howard Theater

BEYOND THE CENTER

Just outside the popular tourist areas are a number of remarkable attractions waiting to be explored. At the top of the list is George Washington's beloved home, Mount Vernon. Kids of all ages love the National Zoo. And who doesn't like an ornate Gothic cathedral whose grotesques include Darth Vader? There are some wonderful parks and gardens too, ranging from the forested trails of Theodore Roosevelt Island to the lushness of the 434-acre (175-ha) National Arboretum and the watery beauty of Kenilworth.

Best for
History, parks, and pandas

Home to
Mount Vernon, National Zoo

Experience
Meeting artists at Old Town Alexandria's Torpedo Factory, and watching whiskey being made at Mount Vernon's distillery

DAYS OUT FROM WASHINGTON, DC

There are a wealth of unique attractions within one to three hours' drive of the city. Experience road trip heaven at Skyline Drive. The Udvar-Hazy Center has all the fabulous air- and spacecraft that the Smithsonian could not fit in their museum on the Mall. Annapolis was briefly the nation's capital, and today is a sailing town with a lot of history and plenty of fine dining. Farther out, the magnificent Colonial Williamsburg site re-creates an 18th-century town with over 100 restored buildings and costumed interpreters.

Best for
Charming historic towns such as Frederick, Middleburg, and Charlottesville

Home to
Colonial Williamsburg, Udvar-Hazy Center, Skyline Drive

Experience
The flight simulators at the Udvar-Hazy Center that let you pilot a fighter jet or blast off into space, and a chat with the reenactors at Colonial Williamsburg

←

1 Planes at the National Air and Space Museum.

2 Calder's *Cheval Rouge* (1974), Sculpture Garden.

3 Van Gogh's *Self Portrait* (1889), National Gallery of Art.

4 Blues Alley, Georgetown.

With its monuments and museums, ravishing restaurants, and sumptuous shopping, Washington is a feast for travelers. These itineraries are intended to be your friend in the city, helping you to see the best that America's capital has to offer.

2 DAYS

Day 1

Morning Start your day rocketing into space on an Apollo mission or soaring at Kitty Hawk on simulators at the National Air and Space Museum (p70). Arrive early and be sure to see the Wright Flyer, the *Spirit of St. Louis*, and the Lunar Module. Afterwards, walk across the Mall to the Sculpture Garden at the National Gallery of Art (p66) to admire works by Chagall and Calder. Enjoy lunch on the patio of the Pavilion Café, overlooking the garden.

Afternoon Spend a couple of leisurely hours strolling around the world and through time at the National Gallery of Art. Choose from Byzantine, Renaissance, and Impressionist collections, or visit the East Wing for modern art. Then walk east along the Mall, then north around the White House (p108). Enjoy the iconic views and linger for a while in Lafayette Square (p112). Then it's back to the Mall and the Lincoln Memorial (p84) to stand at the feet of the statue and read the Gettysburg Address engraved on the wall.

Evening Head to Washington Harbour (p124) and Farmers Fishers Bakers for a farm-to-table dinner. Top off the evening at Gypsy Sally's, one of Georgetown's livelier nightspots, offering a varied menu of blues, rock, and bluegrass music.

Day 2

Morning A stroll through the beautiful, dew-laden Enid A. Haupt Garden is a great way to start the morning before you head across the Mall to the National Museum of Natural History (p74). There is a lot to see here, including the towering dinosaur skeletons, the Hope Diamond (and hundreds of other dazzling gems), and the powerfully reconstructed faces of our early ancestors in the Hall of Human Origins.

Afternoon Pause for lunch at the United States Capitol Cafe, whose gleaming serving stations provide far more delicious fare than its name suggests. If you haven't pre-booked your Capitol (p54) tour online, go to the information booth, where there may still be timed-entry tickets available. After your tour, cool down by strolling through the stunning conservatory and grounds of the US Botanic Garden (p58).

Evening Not far away is the elegant marble building that once housed the *Washington Star* newspaper. Here the Fogo de Chão Brazilian Steakhouse offers paleo-style dining (www.fogodechao.com). Finish your evening at Georgetown's Blues Alley (p125), one of the oldest and most famous jazz venues in the country.

←

1 The plantation house at Mount Vernon.

2 Washington National Cathedral.

3 Old Town Alexandria.

4 Pandas at the National Zoo.

4 DAYS

Day 1

Morning A somber yet uplifting morning awaits at the National Museum of African American History and Culture (*p78*). The exhibits begin underground with slavery, and lighten as you head upwards. Lunch north of the White House with the ultra-fresh fare at Founding Farmers (*www.wearefoundingfarmers.com*).

Afternoon Stroll around the White House (*p108*), taking in the famous views, then celebrate the role of journalism in a free society at the Newseum (*p94*). Inside, be sure to see the 9/11 exhibit, and the gallery where the front pages of 80 global newspapers are displayed daily.

Evening Dine at the Afro-Caribbean Kith and Kin at District Wharf (*p136*). Follow it up with a walk around the Mall's monuments, which are beautifully lit after dark.

Day 2

Morning What better way to start your morning than with a stroll around the Tidal Basin, stopping to explore the Jefferson Memorial (*p85*) and Franklin D. Roosevelt Memorial (*p85*). After, head to the National Museum of American History (*p76*) and the burgers and barbeque at its America's Table restaurant.

Afternoon Time to explore American history: stop to gaze at the (yes, *the*) Star-Spangled Banner. Then walk across the Mall to enjoy the Asian and American art at the Freer Gallery of Art (*p82*).

Evening For dinner, head to Muze, an elegant Asian-fusion restaurant with views of the Washington Channel.

Day 3

Morning Start your day meandering through the sunlit gardens of Mount Vernon (*p162*), George Washington's beloved estate. Enjoy an early lunch at the busy on-site bistro, Mount Vernon Inn, before heading 4 miles (6.5 km) down the road to see the gristmill and distillery, Washington's most successful businesses.

Afternoon Explore charming Old Town Alexandria (*p166*). Start at the Torpedo Factory Art Center, a World War II munitions factory that now houses artists' studios. A stroll around the historic core and some shopping, with a stop for ice cream, rounds off your afternoon.

Evening When you are ready for dinner, head to the elegant, French-inspired Le Refuge for a delicious evening meal (*www.lerefugealexandria.com*).

Day 4

Morning Start at the Gothic Washington National Cathedral (*p164*) with a bit of gargoyle-spotting. Head to the National Zoo (*p160*), and don't miss the golden marmosets that live in the trees. Nearby, 2Amys is the go-to for gourmet pizza.

Afternoon Admire quirky American crafts at the Renwick Gallery (*p113*). Then it's on to the National Archives (*p96*) to view the original Declaration of Independence.

Evening Stroll to the beautiful Union Station (*p59*), and kick back at East Street Café (*www.eaststreetcafe.com*), with its remarkable views of the station's soaring, gilded ceilings, for a relaxing end-of-vacation evening.

Founders and Foundations

The city owes its location to George Washington, who chose the site as the capital. He also participated in the design of the Capitol (p54) and set its cornerstone. Thomas Jefferson also helped design the Capitol, and after the city was burned in 1814, he sold his library to the government to rebuild the Library of Congress (p58).

←

Washington, wearing his Masonic apron, placing the cornerstone of the Capitol

WASHINGTON AS A
PRESIDENTIAL POWERTOWN

Most Americans know stories of their presidents, and many presidents are honored by monuments and memorials in Washington. Where can you follow in the footsteps of legendary presidents, and which of their passions and efforts helped to shape the city we see today?

A PRESIDENTIAL CANAL

Few landmarks have had more presidential attention than the Chesapeake and Ohio Canal (p122). Started by George Washington's Patowmack Company, it had its first spade of earth turned by John Adams. Dwight D. Eisenhower declared the canal a National Monument, while Richard Nixon made it a National Historic Park. The reconstruction of the canal was a milestone of Lyndon Johnson's presidency.

Unfinished Business

In the mid-1800s America was struggling financially, especially after the Civil War. But Ulysses S. Grant saw to it that work was restarted on the Washington Monument (p83), which for years had been just an unfinished stub on the Mall (p62). And the Mall only became the cultural hub it is today when Theodore Roosevelt initiated the completion of L'Enfant's original grand design.

→

Theodore Roosevelt at Washington's Union Station in May 1914

The War Years

During World War II, Franklin D. Roosevelt oversaw the design and construction of the Pentagon *(p170)*, the world's largest office building, which took only 16 months to build. After the war, Harry Truman conceded that the White House *(p108)* was in a terrible state, saying "[t]he damned place is haunted, sure as shootin'." He moved out with his family into a nearby row house while the Executive Mansion was gutted back to the walls and completely re-created, room by room, from scratch.

Did You Know?

The Pentagon has 17 miles (27 km) of corridors and 150 acres (60 ha) of enclosed space.

↑ The Pentagon, built in 1941–2 to house the Department of Defense

The 21st Century

Presidents continue to build and change the US capital. The National Museum of African American History and Culture (NMAAHC) *(p78)* was brought into being by George W. Bush and officially opened by Barack Obama. Not far away, the elegant Old Post Office was purchased and turned into an exclusive hotel by billionaire developer Donald Trump, who, shortly thereafter, became the 45th president of the United States.

Obama speaking at the opening of the NMAAHC ↓

↑ An 1852 plan showing proposed improvements to the Washington Monument

Parks and Paths

From Mount Vernon *(p162)* to Great Falls *(p184)*, the Potomac River is lined with miles of parks and well-groomed trails and paths. The Chesapeake and Ohio Canal *(p122)* towpath follows the river from Georgetown *(p118)* to Great Falls and beyond. On the west bank, the 18-mile (29-km) Mount Vernon Trail passes through Alexandria *(p166)* into Arlington, while on the east side, East Potomac Park *(p145)* is popular with families as well as walkers and cyclists. In the middle of the river, Theodore Roosevelt Island *(p170)* offers miles of hiking trails through the forest.

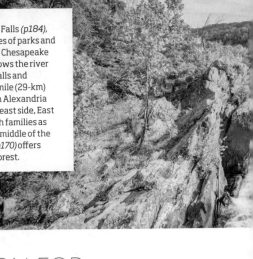

→

Great Falls, a popular hiking area with great views of the river in Mather Gorge

WASHINGTON FOR
THE POTOMAC

Washington has rediscovered its waterfront on a grand scale. Both historic towns such as Georgetown and Alexandria and modern, reinvigorated communities like District Wharf and National Harbor offer a cornucopia of restaurants, shops, parks, and entertainment along the Potomac River.

POTOMAC HISTORY

George Washington envisioned a capital that was both a commercial and political center, and believed its ideal location would be on the river between the port towns of Georgetown and Alexandria. The former was the hub of local commerce through the Civil War, while Alexandria supported trade with England. After the Civil War, and through World War II, the Potomac was lined with gambling barges and floating brothels in what was then an unregulated and tax-free zone. Today, the scenic river is primarily used for recreation.

On the River

A great way to see DC is to rent a kayak, canoe, or scull and enjoy rowing *(p130)* on the river. Cruises are available from Georgetown, Mount Vernon, District Wharf *(p136)*, National Harbor *(p173)*, and Old Town Alexandria, or you can enjoy a less expensive but equally fun ride on a water taxi *(p142)* to all these places as well as Washington Harbour *(p124)* and the Mall *(p62)*.

→

Washington Harbour, a popular place from which to get out on the water

TOP 5 POTOMAC RIVER VIEWS

Iwo Jima Memorial
Spectacular views of the city (p170).

Capital Wheel
Stunning river vistas atop this giant Ferris wheel (p173).

Francis Scott Key Memorial Bridge
🅰 B5
Lovely mid-river views from the Key Bridge.

Mount Vernon
Panoramic views from Washington's grand estate (p162).

Great Falls
Views of wild cascades from the C&O Canal visitor center (p184).

← The wooded Theodore Roosevelt Island, popular with bird-watchers and hikers

Fun on the Waterfront

National Harbor's inviting waterfront has a huge Ferris wheel and hosts festivals and a summer concert series. Street performers, festivals, and parks with picturesque city views are showcased along the river in Old Town Alexandria, while District Wharf boasts a wealth of riverside shops, restaurants, and entertainment alongside the legendary Maine Avenue Fish Market.

↑ The 180-ft- (55-m-) high Capital Wheel at National Harbor

Houses of History

DC has several museums that are all about the African-American experience. One of the Smithsonian's hottest venues is the remarkable National Museum of African American History and Culture *(p78)*. The home of Frederick Douglass is now a National Historic Site *(p172)*, while the Mary McLeod Bethune Council House National Historic Site *(p153)* preserves the legacy of the legendary educator and activist.

→

The Serenity Room at the National Museum of African American History and Culture

Did You Know?

By 1804, all Northern states had voted to abolish slavery, and in 1850, DC ended slave auctions.

WASHINGTON FOR
BLACK HISTORY

Washington holds a unique place in African-American history. After Lincoln's Emancipation Proclamation in 1863, the city became a sanctuary for free black people and slaves who had managed to escape. It was a hub of political action and protest throughout the Civil Rights era. Washington has been home to renowned African-Americans, including abolitionist and statesman Frederick Douglass, legendary jazzman Duke Ellington, and Barack Obama, who became the country's first African-American president in 2009.

Memorials and Monuments

Several DC monuments pay tribute to African-Americans. The Lincoln Memorial *(p84)* has been the backdrop for several civil rights events, including the iconic "I Have a Dream" speech by Dr. Martin Luther King, Jr., who has been honored at the Martin Luther King, Jr. Memorial *(p84)*. Also of note is the African American Civil War Memorial *(p153)*, which honors the 200,000 African-American troops that fought in the nation's bloodiest conflict.

←

Martin Luther King, Jr. Memorial, Tidal Basin

MARIAN ANDERSON SINGS AT THE LINCOLN MEMORIAL

The Daughters of the American Revolution rescinded the celebrated singer's invitation to perform when their membership objected to hosting a black woman. First Lady Eleanor Roosevelt cancelled her DAR membership and arranged to have Anderson sing in front of an audience of 75,000 from the steps of the Lincoln Memorial.

→
Mary McLeod Bethune, renowned educator and civil and women's rights activist

Frederick Douglass Memorial Hall, Howard University ↓

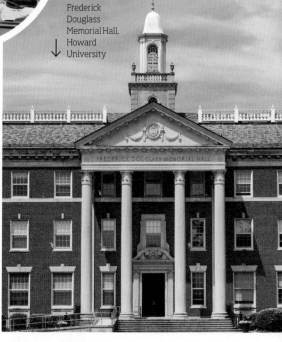

Cultural Touchstones

The Lincoln Theatre *(p157)*, a mainstay of the "Black Broadway" in the 1930s and 40s, today presents an array of multicultural entertainment. Howard University *(p152)*, one of the country's first institutes of higher learning for black people, is now a top choice for African-Americans enrolled in prestigious science, technology, engineering, and math (STEM) programs.

George Washington Fires his City Planner

Pierre L'Enfant created a city plan with broad avenues and lots of public spaces and parks. Developers were annoyed, as over half the available land could not be built upon. When L'Enfant tore down a city commissioner's new mansion that had been built in one of his planned sight lines, he became the first Federal employee to be fired.

←

L'Enfant planning the city with Washington

WASHINGTON FOR
SCANDALS

DC has a long history of curious and bizarre scandals. As appropriate for a city whose reason for existence is political power, the scandals reflect the history of the place itself, with even incidents that were tragic in nature often containing an element of humor.

TOP 3 OTHER PRESIDENTS IN HOT WATER

John F. Kennedy
Rumors of multiple affairs, including one with actress and sex symbol Marilyn Monroe, were damaging to Kennedy's presidency.

Richard Nixon
America's best known scandal, Watergate (p115) eventually led Richard Nixon to resign to avoid impeachment.

Donald Trump
Trump's administration has been haunted by constant allegations of collusion in the Russian scheme to influence the 2016 US presidential election in his favor.

Thomas Jefferson and Sally Hemings

During his presidency, rumors circulated that Jefferson had had an affair with one of his slaves, the young Sally Hemings, which lasted for years and produced several children. Although Jefferson always denied the affair, DNA testing in 1998 proved that he was the father of her children.

→

Caricature of Jefferson and Hemings dated around 1804

The British Set Fire to Washington

In 1814, during the War of 1812, British forces entered Washington and set fire to several buildings. First Lady Dolley Madison had fled the White House just ahead of the invading troops. She left behind a fine feast laid out for what she had hoped would be her husband and officers of the victorious US army. The British troops devoured the feast, drank the wine, and then set fire to the White House and several other city buildings.

→

Illustration depicting the burning of the city during the War of 1812

Burr Shoots Hamilton

In 1804, Vice President Aaron Burr killed former Treasury Secretary Alexander Hamilton in a duel. No murder charge was ever brought. After his term, Burr went west, acquired more than 1,550 sq miles (4,000 sq km) of land, and began collecting men and arms, purportedly to start his own country. Jefferson arrested him for treason, but he was eventually let go on a technicality.

←

Burr shooting Hamilton in a duel

Bill Clinton and Monica Lewinsky

Bill Clinton's ill-advised affair with 22-year-old intern Monica Lewinsky led to his being only the second president in US history to be impeached, after Andrew Johnson in 1868. The details spread quickly across the world as the internet became commercially accessible for the first time. Clinton was later judged not guilty by the Senate and finished his term as the 42nd president.

→

Monica Lewinsky and Bill Clinton pictured together at the White House

Ponds in the Constitution
Gardens reflecting the
Washington Monument ↑

WASHINGTON FOR
GARDENS AND GREEN SPACES

Washington's beautiful parks and gardens are one of its hidden delights.
You are never far from a place with cool green shade, fountains, flowers,
and inviting benches. There are traditional gardens bursting with color,
lovely parks with paths and ponds, special-purpose green spaces like the
National Arboretum, and beloved outdoor venues like the National Zoo.

Fabulous Flowers

Flowers, flowers everywhere.
The 1920s gardens of Dumbarton
Oaks *(p125)* are elegant and
lovely, with an air of Victorian
mystery. Mount Vernon *(p162)*
has re-created the gardens that
George Washington would have
enjoyed, and the entire Capitol
Grounds are a large, park-like
space with the US Botanic Garden
(p58) at its center. But perhaps
the ultimate Washington garden
experience is an early springtime
walk along the edge of the Tidal
Basin *(p85)*, under the arched,
blooming branches of the
exquisite cherry trees.

→

Flowering plants and
greenhouses at the
US Botanic Garden

Shaded Green Spaces

A wealth of green spaces offer moments of quietude and beauty. On the Mall (p62), a tranquil pond, its edges traced by tree-shaded paths, is the centerpiece of Constitution Gardens. Along the Potomac, Georgetown Waterfront Park (p131) is a bustling family-friendly space, while away from the river to the north, Rock Creek Park (p171) boasts a stream-side path that is a favorite with walkers, joggers, and cyclists.

← Kids enjoying a cooling water feature at the Georgetown Waterfront Park

TOP 4 LITTLE-KNOWN GARDENS

Bishop's Garden
A lovely walled garden outside the National Cathedral (p164).

Lady Bird Johnson Park
🅿 C9
Flower-filled park stretching along the banks of the Potomac.

Enid A. Haupt Garden
Blossom-laden park set behind the Smithsonian Castle (p80).

Hirshhorn Sculpture Garden
Tranquil walled garden opposite the Hirshhorn Museum (p81) with magnificent sculptures.

🔍 HIDDEN GEM
Pershing Park

Surrounded by busy streets, Pershing Park is a secluded, watery sanctuary a block from the White House.

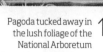

Pagoda tucked away in ↑ the lush foliage of the National Arboretum

Parks with Purpose

Washington has a number of park-like spaces that have a purpose beyond beauty. Chief among them is the National Arboretum (p172), whose 446 acres (180 ha), while a research space for botanists, are simply a magnificent green space filled with trees and flower-lined paths for visitors. The National Zoo (p160) is a glorious park and a favorite with kids, but it is also a respected conservation center and home to endangered species such as scimitar-horned oryx and red pandas.

All American

Art that expresses the American experience is huge in Washington. Two of the best places to engage with immersive contemporary art are the Renwick Gallery *(p113)* and the Smithsonian American Art Museum *(p92)*. The latter holds an extraordinary piece by Nam June Paik called *Electronic Superhighway*, a 50-channel video installation. The National Portrait Gallery *(p92)* holds paintings and images of Americans who have played an influential role in the country's history.

 HIDDEN GEM
The Art of Bonsai and Penjing

Tranquility and beauty prevail in the pavilions and gardens of the National Bonsai and Penjing Museum at the National Arboretum *(p172)*. These timeless masterpieces of artistically styled miniature living trees are known as bonsai in Japan and penjing in China.

Electronic Superhighway (1995) at the Smithsonian American Art Museum ↑

WASHINGTON FOR
ART LOVERS

Washington is one of the nation's stellar art and culture destinations, its museums and galleries displaying some of the most dazzling collections in the country. Alongside this, the performing arts scene offers world-class recitals and shows as well as cutting-edge theater in small venues.

Dazzling Masterpieces

The acclaimed National Gallery of Art *(p66)* holds European and American masterpieces in a variety of media by such artists as Leonardo da Vinci, Titian, Raphael, Monet, Rubens, Rembrandt, and Rodin. The Smithsonian's Arthur M. Sackler Gallery *(p81)* has an exceptional collection of Indian and Asian artwork, including ancient Chinese jade and bronze, while the National Museum of African Art *(p81)* has some excellent examples of ancient African art on display.

←

Admiring portraits at the National Gallery of Art

TOP 5 MUST-SEE MUSEUMS

National Gallery of Art
World-class European and American art (p66).

The Phillips Collection
America's first museum of modern art (p150).

SAAM and the Renwick Gallery
DC's favorite art museums (p113).

Arthur M. Sackler Gallery
Contemporary and ancient Asian art (p81).

National Museum of African Art
The first US museum for African art (p81).

Modern and Contemporary

The Phillips Collection (p150) boasts art by Renoir, O'Keefe, Klee, and Rothko. Edgy, innovative, and unique art is on display at the Hirshhorn Museum (p81), while the National Gallery of Art showcases works by artists such as Miro, Moore, and Calder.

→

Renoir's *Luncheon of the Boating Party* (1881), Phillips Collection

Performing Arts

The nation's busiest performing arts center, the Kennedy Center (p115) in Georgetown features top music, dance, and theatrical events on its nine stages. To experience cutting-edge, experimental performances in an intimate setting, head to the Woolly Mammoth Theatre on D Street in Penn Quarter, while the best of Broadway is available at the National Theatre (p99).

→

Bust of John F. Kennedy at the Kennedy Center

Mini Memorials

Spend a fun day locating and enjoying some of DC's dozens of lesser-known memorials. The warm, inviting figure of Einstein in front of the National Academy of Sciences at 22nd St and Constitution Avenue, NW is popular with children, who like to climb up into his lap. The George Mason Memorial at the Tidal Basin is a lovely spot with gardens, a fountain, and a statue of a relaxed Mason sitting on a bench. Mason became known as the forgotten Founding Father because he played a large role in crafting the new Constitution but refused to sign it as, among other things, it did not end the slave trade. The Titanic Memorial on the Southwest waterfront at P Street, SW was erected by the surviving women passengers to honor the men who stayed behind.

$\rightarrow$

Enjoying climbing up the Albert Einstein Memorial

WASHINGTON OFF THE
BEATEN PATH

Washington has so many world-renowned attractions that some smaller sites get overlooked. All gems in their own right, they tell important stories, like the forgotten Founding Father, why George Washington kept a distillery, or the terrible but inspiring tale of the medicine of war.

Hidden History

Some small sites tell big stories. In Silver Spring, Maryland, the National Museum of Health and Medicine focuses on the study of anatomic anomalies, medical curiosities, and military injuries (older kids love it). Washington's distillery at Mount Vernon *(p162)* was once his most successful business. Along with the neighboring gristmill, it has been rebuilt, and visitors can watch whiskey being made as it was in Washington's day.

Did You Know?

With dinner at the Inn at Mount Vernon, you can taste whiskeys from Washington's distillery.

↑ George Washington's distillery, Mount Vernon

← Guided tours taking in the displays at the National Museum of Health and Medicine

It's All in the Timing

Sometimes it's not about where, but when. A stroll around the west end of the Mall *(p62)* after twilight, when all the paths and monuments are beautifully lit, is a little-known treat for visitors. On some balmy summer evenings, there are free movies shown on giant open-air screens near the Washington Monument *(p83)*. Across town, the H Street Corridor *(p100)* is one of the city's trendiest after-dark venues, offering creative dining and great entertainment and nightlife.

←
The World War II Memorial, Washington Monument, and the Mall beautifully illuminated at night

TOP 5 LITTLE-KNOWN SITES

Heurich House
◉ E4 ⌂ 1307 New Hampshire Ave NW ⬡ heurichhouse.org
Home of 19th-century city brewmaster Christian Heurich.

Kahlil Gibran Memorial
◉ C2 ⌂ 3100 Massachusetts Ave NW
Sculptural wall and garden dedicated to the poet and philosopher.

The Awakening
National Harbor sculpture emerging from the earth *(p173)*.

Mansion on O Street
◉ E4 ⌂ 2020 O St NW
Eclectic mansion with secret passages.

DEA Museum
◉ P4 ⌂ 700 Army Navy Dr
Arlington museum on the history of drug use.

WASHINGTON FOR
FAMILIES

With museums packed with cool stuff, scores of parks, and space to run, play, and fly kites on the Mall, Washington is one of the best cities in the US for kids to learn about the history of the country, be exposed to the most advanced science and technology in the world, and just have fun.

Just Plain Fun

In National Harbor (p173), The Awakening, a statue of a giant emerging from the earth, is popular with youngsters, who climb all over it. Nearby, the Capital Wheel whisks them 180 ft (55 m) above the river for thrills and incredible views. Another favorite is the International Spy Museum (p140), where kids create cover stories and become a spy for a day. And at the end of the day, a paddleboat ride around the Tidal Basin (p85) is a great way to wind down.

→

Kids having fun at the International Spy Museum

The Greatest Outdoors

The National Zoo *(p160)* is a huge, park-like space that just happens to have giraffes, pandas, and thousands of other animals, all in natural enclosures. The National Arboretum *(p172)* is a vast garden with a great tram tour and places to let off steam while learning about trees. And nothing is better than flying a kite on the Mall near the Washington Monument *(p83)* – breezy spring and fall are best, and kites are available in most museum gift shops.

← Kids enjoying the National Zoo, and flying a kite on the Mall *(inset)*

TOP
5
MORE GREAT TIMES FOR KIDS

National Museum of American History
Treasure trove of Americana including Kermit the Frog *(p76)*.

Oxon Hill Farm
Great for feeding farm animals and learning about rural life *(p173)*.

Canal Boat Tour
Boat trips start from the Great Falls Visitor Center *(p184)*.

Bike and Bus Tours
Rides on open top tour buses *(p196)*, and bike tours on the Mall.

Newseum
A teleprompter and live camera for kids to play newsreader *(p94)*.

The Coolest History

You can't take two steps in any of the major museums without hearing someone say "awesome!" Heading up the list is the Museum of Natural History *(p74)*, where kids can handle giant bugs and gaze into the toothy grin of a Tyrannosaurus rex. The nearby Air and Space Museum *(p70)*, home to the first television model of the *Enterprise*, also has wow-power. Mount Vernon *(p162)* offers a fun horse-drawn wagon ride around Pioneer Farm.

↑ Tyrannosaurus rex at the National Museum of Natural History

Tour America's Government

Many of Washington, DC's beautiful government buildings are filled with historical significance and amazing art, and are open for free tours. These include the National Archives (p96), the United States Capitol (p54), the White House (p108), and the Library of Congress (p58), the world's largest archive.

←

Magnificently decorated interior of the Library of Congress

WASHINGTON ON A
SHOESTRING

Washington's amazing variety of free attractions ensure that visitors will never run out of things to see and do. Free museums, tours, and green spaces keep visitors active during the day, while theater and film festivals and music performances make evenings a delight.

TOP 5 FREE SIGHTS

US Capitol
Grand space with the Brumidi Corridors and a stunning rotunda (p54).

The Mall and Memorial Parks
DC's central feature, with several memorials and monuments (p82).

National Gallery of Art
One of the most visited galleries in the US (p66).

Smithsonian Museums
A collection of 18 fascinating museums and galleries (p70).

National Archives
Home to the nation's most important historical documents (p96).

Festivals and Events

The capital is packed with such an incredible variety of free festivals and events it can be hard to choose just a few. There are performances every day on the Millennium Stage at the Kennedy Center *(p115)*, ranging from comedy and the spoken word to dance and all forms of music. The National Gallery of Art *(p66)* holds the open-air Jazz in the Garden series every Friday in summer, while the DC Jazz Festival *(p42)* includes free concerts alongside ticketed ones. The Shakespeare Theatre Company's Free For All *(p43)* is a much-loved city tradition, offering performances of the Bard's works each summer. Foodies will enjoy the free tastings at the Giant National Capital Barbecue Battle in June, while film buffs can choose between the NoMa Summer Screen, Movie Nights in Chinatown Park, and Films at the Stone.

→

Band performing at the DC Jazz Festival

Gardens, Galleries, and Museums

Washington is a city filled with glorious green spaces, magnificent art, and amazing artifacts. The US Botanic Garden *(p58)* offers serene beauty, while the National Arboretum *(p172)* has breathtaking azalea gardens. On rainy days head indoors to the National Gallery of Art, the Smithsonian's 18 acclaimed museums, or any of the dozens of other world-class government and private museums that are free to enter and guaranteed to engross.

↑ Robert Indiana's *AMOR* at the National Gallery of Art *(inset)*, and the US Botanic Garden

A YEAR IN
WASHINGTON, DC

JANUARY

△ **Restaurant Week** *(mid-Jan)*. Many of the city's top restaurants offer fixed price specials for lunch or dinner.

Martin Luther King, Jr. Day *(3rd Mon)*. Commemorative events are held at the Martin Luther King, Jr. Memorial, Washington National Cathedral, Kennedy Center, and others.

FEBRUARY

Black History Month *(throughout)*. Theater, dance, music, visual arts, and spoken word events.

△ **Chinese New Year** *(1st fortnight)*. Enjoy parades, dancing, and live music at N St, Chinatown.

Presidents' Day Weekend *(3rd Mon)*. All past presidents are honored at multiple events, such as the George Washington Birthday Parade.

MAY

Washington National Cathedral Flower Mart *(1st Fri)*. Flower and gift booths and music on offer.

Around the World Embassy Tour *(1st Sat)*. Over 40 embassies welcome visitors and provide cultural events and experiences.

△ **Memorial Day** *(last Mon)*. Wreath-laying, speeches, and music honor war veterans at city memorials and Arlington National Cemetery.

JUNE

Capital Pride *(early Jun)*. A street festival and parade celebrate the LGBT+ communities of DC.

DC Jazz Festival *(mid-Jun)*. This two-week festival attracts the best musicians from across the US.

△ **Smithsonian Folklife Festival** *(late Jun–early Jul)*. This huge celebration of folk culture includes music, dance, games, and food on the Mall.

SEPTEMBER

△ **Labor Day Weekend Concert** *(Sun before Labor Day)*. The National Symphony Orchestra performs on the West Lawn of the Capitol.

H Street Festival *(mid-Sep)*. This spirited block party offers food stalls, art, and performances on 14 stages.

Fiesta DC *(late Sep)*. A colorful parade and festival celebrate Latino culture.

OCTOBER

△ **Annapolis Boat Shows** *(mid-Oct)*. World's largest sailboat and powerboat shows with in-water boat access, workshops and exhibits.

White House Fall Garden Tours *(mid-Oct)*. Visits to the Rose Garden, Jacqueline Kennedy Garden, Children's Garden, and the South Lawn are on offer.

Boo at the Zoo *(end Oct)*. A Halloween celebration for children at the National Zoo with treats, education, and live entertainment.

MARCH

St. Patrick's Day *(Sun before Mar 17)*. A parade to celebrate Irish culture on Constitution Avenue, NW.

△ **Blossom Kite Festival** *(last Sat)*. Kite enthusiasts gather near the Washington Monument on the Mall to fly their kites and compete for prizes.

National Cherry Blossom Festival *(late Mar–mid-Apr)*. A parade and festivities celebrate the blooming of Washington's famous cherry trees.

APRIL

△ **White House Easter Egg Roll** *(Easter Mon)*. Children's egg races and entertainment.

Truckeroo *(Apr–Sep)*. This one-Friday-a-month food truck event also features live music.

Filmfest DC *(late Apr–early May)*. New films from around the world plus film-oriented events.

JULY

Military Band Concert Series *(Jun–Aug)*. Free concerts are held at the Capitol and military memorials on most evenings.

△ **Independence Day** *(Jul 4)*. A free concert at the Capitol, a parade along Constitution Avenue, and fireworks on the Mall. Old Town Alexandria and Mount Vernon have parades and fireworks.

Capital Fringe Festival *(last 3 weeks)*. More than 100 independent theater, dance, music, art and other live performances take place.

AUGUST

△ **Arlington County Fair** *(mid-Aug)*. A lively fair with food, crafts, music, and fairground rides.

Summer Restaurant Week *(mid-Aug)*. More than 250 restaurants offer fixed-price dinners, brunches, and lunches.

Free for All *(late Aug–early Sep)*. This popular annual summer event sees free nightly performances of the Bard's classic plays by the Shakespeare Theater Company.

NOVEMBER

Veterans Day *(Nov 11)*. Wreath-laying, services, and concerts take place at Arlington National Cemetery and various city memorials to honor veterans.

△ **Sculpture Garden Ice Rink** *(mid-Nov–Mar)*. The pond at the National Gallery of Art's Sculpture Garden becomes a popular ice rink each winter.

Kennedy Center Holiday Festival *(late Nov–New Year's Eve)*. Enjoy musicals, ballet, and classical concerts for the holiday season.

DECEMBER

ZooLights *(late Nov–Jan 1)*. Thousands of light sculptures portray the popular animals, alongside activities and live entertainment.

Christmas at Mount Vernon *(late Nov–early Jan)*. Experience an 18th-century Christmas at Mount Vernon, George Washington's plantation.

△ **National Christmas Tree** *(throughout)*. The decorated National Christmas Tree, and 56 state and territory trees, stand in the Ellipse near the White House. Live entertainment nightly.

1

A BRIEF
HISTORY

Washington was designed from the ground up to be the capital, with wide avenues, lush parks, and grand buildings. Over the years it has also been a thriving port, an urban fortress in the bloody Civil War, a safe harbor for fleeing slaves, and, after World War II, a flourishing center of arts and culture.

A Meeting of Civilizations and Colonization

Archaic Indians were the first humans to occupy the region, about 6,000 years ago. By the time English soldier John Smith arrived in 1607, the Powhatan tribe was living in the region. The 1614 marriage of settler John Rolfe and Pocahontas, daughter of the Powhatan chief, kept the peace for a few years until a formal agreement in 1646. Some 100 years after the arrival of the first settlers, frustration grew over British rule. The Declaration of Independence was issued on July 4, 1776, leading to a long and bloody revolution that ended in 1781 with the surrender of the British. George Washington was unanimously elected president.

1 A map of the city in its early days. ↑

2 British troops setting fire to the city during the War of 1812.

3 Lee surrendering to Grant at Appomattox.

4 John Booth shooting Abraham Lincoln in 1865.

Timeline of events

1751
The small tobacco port of Georgetown is founded.

1789
George Washington is unanimously elected the first president of the United States for the first of two terms.

1793
Washington lays the cornerstone of the Capitol, wearing his Masonic apron.

1800
The Federal government moves from Philadelphia to Washington.

1812
The War of 1812 with the British begins on June 18.

A New City

In 1778, Washington selected this area as a capital. He chose surveyor Andrew Ellicott and his assistant Benjamin Banneker, a free African-American man, to lay out the streets, and asked his old friend Major Pierre Charles L'Enfant to create a grand city plan *(p85)*. L'Enfant borrowed heavily from Europe, incorporating broad, tree-lined avenues and large green spaces. In 1800 the government moved to the city, which was still a near wilderness, with mud streets and roaming farm animals. Nonetheless, John Adams took up residence in the new President's House.

A Tale of Two Wars

New tensions with Britain escalated in 1812, and America declared war. In August 1814, British troops reached the city and set fire to numerous buildings. Over the next few decades, the city reflected the nation's growing tensions over slavery. In 1860, following the election of Abraham Lincoln, many southern states seceded from the Union, launching the Civil War. On April 9, 1865, Confederate General Robert E. Lee surrendered, but on April 14 disaffected Confederate actor John Wilkes Booth shot President Lincoln at Ford's Theatre.

CAMP WASHINGTON

On April 12, 1861, shots were fired on Fort Sumter and the Civil War began. By summer, 50,000 army volunteers had arrived in Washington, and the city found itself in the business of housing, feeding, and clothing them, as well as caring for the wounded. Among those who came to help were author Louisa May Alcott and poet Walt Whitman.

1814

The British set fire to several Washington buildings during the War of 1812.

1829

Englishman John Smithson leaves his fortune to the people of America for the establishment of the Smithsonian Institution.

1862

Slavery is abolished in the city, making it the first place in America to free its slaves.

1867

General Oliver Otis Howard helps establish the African-American Howard University.

A New Century

In 1901, participation in the "city beautiful" movement led to massive urban development and a huge advance for L'Enfant's grand plan. When the US entered World War I in 1917, women came to the city to fill the posts vacated by men, and suffragists took to the streets to campaign for women's right to vote. Meanwhile, segregation continued, with African-Americans banned from voting and discriminated against in housing and education. The 1920s, however, were a period of commercial, artistic, and literary success for the black community, with the area around U Street attracting creative African-Americans.

The New Deal and World War II

Following the stock market crash of 1929, President Roosevelt created the "New Deal," an ambitious program that paid people to undertake public works, from planting trees on the Mall to completing city buildings such as the National Gallery of Art and Supreme Court. After the US entered World War II in 1941, Washington's population soared. Once again, women from all across the country arrived in the capital, eager to take on government jobs while the men were overseas.

↑ *We Can Do It!*, a poster that became a symbol of female empowerment

Timeline of events

1920
With the adoption of the 19th Amendment, women gain the right to vote.

1929
After years of runaway speculation, the stock market crashes, starting the Great Depression.

1932
Calling themselves the "Bonus Army," 17,000 mostly jobless World War I veterans and another 26,000 protesters march on Washington.

1941
Construction begins on the Pentagon. A few months later, America enters World War II.

Civil Rights and a New Era

After the Supreme Court passed strong anti-discrimination laws, life in the city began to change. On August 28, 1963, Martin Luther King, Jr. led the March on Washington to support civil rights, and from the steps of the Lincoln Memorial shared his dream in words that would echo for generations *(p101)*. In November, the nation was stunned by the assassination of John F. Kennedy, and five years later, on April 4, 1968, by that of the 39-year-old Dr. King, today revered as a hero and martyr.

Washington, DC Today

The terrorist attacks on September 11, 2001 on New York and Washington forever altered life in America's capital, creating a heightened need for security that is felt by residents and visitors alike. In 2009, Barack Obama became the first African-American president in US history. Walking down Pennsylvania Avenue after his inauguration, he entered the White House – a building originally built by slave labor – as the leader of a great nation. And while much is left to be done in striving for equality for all, it seems likely that the Founding Fathers would be pleased with this remarkable moment in Washington's journey.

1 Suffragists inviting people to protest, 1917.

2 National Gallery of Art being built, 1939.

3 Dr. King at the 1963 March on Washington.

4 President Obama at his inauguration, 2009.

Did You Know?
Theodore Roosevelt was shot at in 1912, but the bullet was slowed by a 50-page speech in his coat pocket.

1968
Riots break out and blocks of Washington are burned.

1971
The *Washington Post* publishes the Pentagon Papers.

1976
The Metro opens with just one route, five stations, and 4.6 miles (7.5 km) of track. Today, it has six routes, 91 stations, and 117 miles (188 km) of track.

2014
Marijuana is legalized in the District of Columbia.

2017
Donald Trump takes office as the 45th US president.

EXPERIENCE

The interior of the Jefferson Memorial

...AVE SWORN

WE HOLD THESE TRUTHS TO BE SELF-
EVIDENT, THAT ALL MEN ARE CREATED
EQUAL, THAT THEY ARE ENDOWED BY THEIR
CREATOR WITH CERTAIN INALIENABLE
RIGHTS, AMONG THESE ARE LIFE, LIBERTY
AND THE PURSUIT OF HAPPINESS, THAT
TO SECURE THESE RIGHTS GOVERNMENTS
ARE INSTITUTED AMONG MEN, WE ...
SOLEMNLY PUBLISH AND DECLARE, THAT
THESE COLONIES ARE AND OF RIGHT
OUGHT TO BE FREE AND INDEPENDENT
STATES —AND FOR THE SUPPORT OF THIS
DECLARATION, WITH A FIRM RELIANCE
ON THE PROTECTION OF DIVINE
PROVIDENCE, WE MUTUALLY PLEDGE
OUR LIVES, OUR FORTUNES AND OUR
SACRED HONOUR.

CAPITOL HILL

Soon after the Constitution was ratified in 1788, America's seat of government began to take root on Capitol Hill. The site was chosen in 1791 from 10 acres (4 ha) that were ceded by the state of Maryland. Town planner Major Pierre Charles L'Enfant chose a hill on the east side of the area as the foundation for the Capitol building and the center of the new city. In more than 200 years, Capitol Hill has developed into a bustling microcosm of modern America. Symbols of the country's cultural development are everywhere, from its Federal buildings to its centers of commerce, shops, and restaurants, as well as its multicultural residential areas. The Capitol Hill area is frequented by the most powerful people in the United States. While access to official government buildings is strictly controlled for reasons of security, ordinary citizens may still find members of Congress greeting tour groups in the halls of the Capitol or dining at local restaurants.

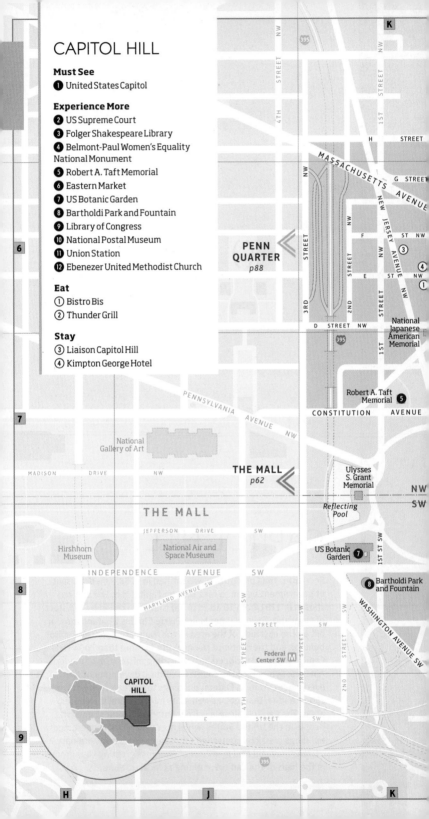

CAPITOL HILL

Must See

1 United States Capitol

Experience More

2 US Supreme Court
3 Folger Shakespeare Library
4 Belmont-Paul Women's Equality National Monument
5 Robert A. Taft Memorial
6 Eastern Market
7 US Botanic Garden
8 Bartholdi Park and Fountain
9 Library of Congress
10 National Postal Museum
11 Union Station
12 Ebenezer United Methodist Church

Eat

1 Bistro Bis
2 Thunder Grill

Stay

3 Liaison Capitol Hill
4 Kimpton George Hotel

PENN QUARTER p88

THE MALL p62

National Japanese American Memorial

Robert A. Taft Memorial **5**

CONSTITUTION AVENUE

Ulysses S. Grant Memorial

Reflecting Pool

NW / SW

US Botanic Garden **7**

Bartholdi Park and Fountain **8**

National Gallery of Art

MADISON DRIVE NW

THE MALL

JEFFERSON DRIVE SW

Hirshhorn Museum

National Air and Space Museum

INDEPENDENCE AVENUE SW

MARYLAND AVENUE SW

Federal Center SW

CAPITOL HILL

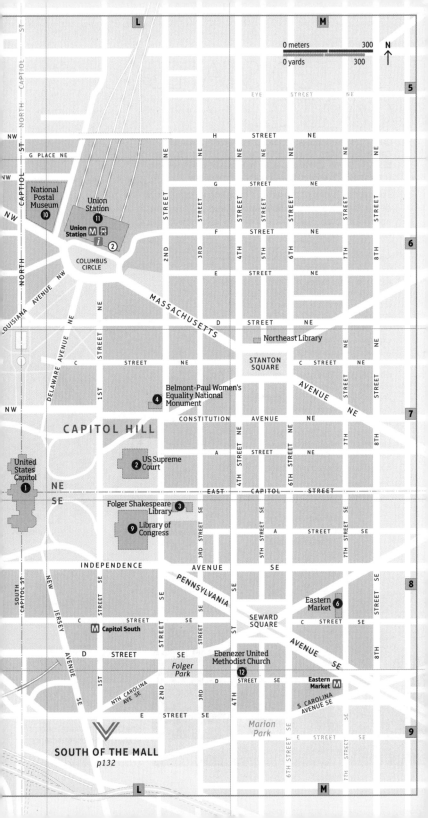

① 🛝 🍴 🛍️

UNITED STATES CAPITOL

📍K7 🏛️ Main entrance: beneath East Front Plaza at 1st & East Capitol Sts Ⓜ Capitol South, Union Station, Federal Center SW 🚌 32, 34, 36, 96 🕐 8:30am–4:30pm Mon–Sat (check website for details) 🚫 Federal hols 🌐 visitthecapitol.gov

The Capitol is one of the world's best-known symbols of democracy. Every year about four million visitors come to admire the breathtaking building and learn how America creates and passes the laws that govern the nation.

Since 1793, when George Washington laid the cornerstone, the Neo-Classical Capitol has been under almost constant renovation. In 2008 the vast visitor center opened, welcoming visitors to the building's stunning interior, with its vaulted ceilings, exquisite tile- and woodwork, and expansive art-filled spaces. While waiting for a free tour (book ahead), visitors can explore the Exhibition Hall, where artifacts and original documents tell the story of Congress and the Capitol Building. There are also videos, models, and interactive computers, as well as two theaters showing the proceedings in the House and Senate Chambers. The Emancipation Hall honors the enslaved laborers who helped build the Capitol building.

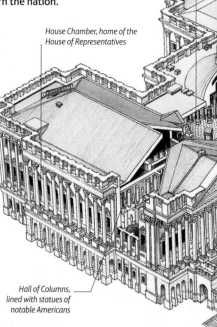

National Statuary Hall, with two statues from each state

House Chamber, home of the House of Representatives

→

The United States Capitol building, the legislative heart of Washington

Hall of Columns, lined with statues of notable Americans

Did You Know?
___

When the two Chambers of Congress are in session, the viewing galleries are open to the public.

←

The Capitol, marking the center of the city, whose quadrants are defined by a point directly below the building's dome

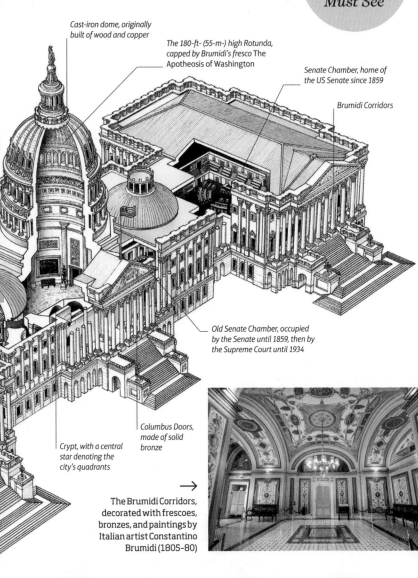

Cast-iron dome, originally built of wood and copper

The 180-ft- (55-m-) high Rotunda, capped by Brumidi's fresco The Apotheosis of Washington

Senate Chamber, home of the US Senate since 1859

Brumidi Corridors

Old Senate Chamber, occupied by the Senate until 1859, then by the Supreme Court until 1934

Columbus Doors, made of solid bronze

Crypt, with a central star denoting the city's quadrants

→ The Brumidi Corridors, decorated with frescoes, bronzes, and paintings by Italian artist Constantino Brumidi (1805–80)

1791
△ George Washington selects the site for the Capitol; later, William Thornton wins a contest to design the building.

1814
△ During the War of 1812 the British burn down the Capitol; it is again damaged by fire in 1851 and 1898.

1958
△ A major expansion of the Capitol building starts with a 32-ft (10-m) extension of the east front.

2008
△ A sleek underground visitor center opens to the public after eight years of construction.

EXPERIENCE MORE

2

US Supreme Court

📍L7 🏛1st St between E Capitol St & Maryland Ave, NE Ⓜ Capitol South ⏰9am–4:30pm Mon–Fri 🚫Federal hols 🌐supreme court.gov

Emblazoned with the motto "Equal Justice Under Law," this elegant Corinthian building was designed by Cass Gilbert and opened in 1935. Sculptures depicting the allegorical figures of the *Contemplation of Justice* and the *Guardian of the Law* stand beside the steps while above the entrance are figures of John Marshall (far right) and William Howard Taft (far left), the fourth and tenth US Chief Justices respectively.

The Supreme Court forms the judicial and third branch of the US government, providing the highest ruling in the nation's legal disputes and issues of constitutionality. All oral arguments are open to the public, but admission is on a first-come, first-served basis, and seating is limited. When not in session, public lectures on the court are held every hour on the half-hour in the courtroom (check details on the website).

> 💬 INSIDER TIP
> **Legal Drama**
>
> To watch the Supreme Court in action, arrive well before the 9:30am seating and pick either the queue for a full one-hour argument or for a three-minute slot.

3

Folger Shakespeare Library

📍L8 🏛201 E Capitol St, SE Ⓜ Capitol South ⏰10am–5pm Mon–Sat, noon–5pm Sun 🚫Federal hols 🌐folger.edu

Inspired by Shakespeare's own era, this library and museum celebrate the works and times of the Elizabethan playwright.

The research library was a gift to the American people in 1932 from Henry Clay Folger who, as a student in 1874, began to collect Shakespeare's works. Folger funded the construction of this edifice, built specifically to house his collection. It contains 310,000 Elizabethan books and manuscripts, as well as the world's largest collection of the Bard's writings, including a third of the surviving copies of the 1623 First Folio (first editions of Shakespeare's works).

The Folger hosts cultural events such as regular performances of the Bard's plays in a 250-seat reconstruction of an Elizabethan theater.

In the library grounds, the Elizabethan Garden has plants that are featured in Shakespeare's plays. The playwright's birthday is marked every April with jugglers, music, theater shows, and a tour of the library.

4

Belmont-Paul Women's Equality National Monument

📍L7 🏛144 Constitution Ave, NE Ⓜ Capitol South, Union Station ⏰9am–5pm Wed–Sun 🚫Federal hols 🌐nps.gov/bepa

A stately historic home, this is also a museum dedicated

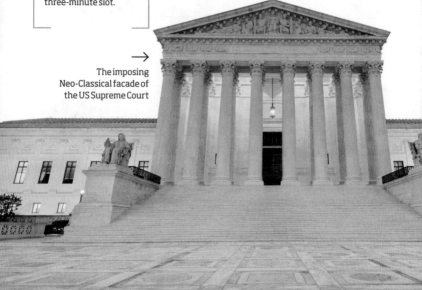

→ The imposing Neo-Classical facade of the US Supreme Court

 A kaleidoscopic display of some of the fresh produce on offer at Eastern Market

to the story of the women's suffrage and equal rights movements. Since 1929, it has been the headquarters of the National Women's Party, who won the right for American women to vote in 1920. Today, visitors can admire the period furnishings and suffragist artifacts, including the desk on which Alice Paul, the leader of the party, wrote the, as yet unratified, Equal Rights Amendment of 1923.

A century earlier, in the early 1800s, the house was the home of Albert Gallatin, the Treasury Secretary under President Thomas Jefferson. It was here that Gallatin entertained a number of wealthy contributors whose financial backing brought about the Louisiana Purchase in 1803, which doubled the size of the United States.

 5

Robert A. Taft Memorial

Q K7 **A** Constitution Ave & 1st St, NW **M** Union Station **w** aoc.gov

In a park opposite the US Capitol stands this statue of Ohio senator Robert A. Taft (1889–1953). The son of the 27th US president William Howard Taft, Robert was a Republican, famous for

sponsoring the Taft-Hartley Act, the regulator of collective bargaining between labor and management. The memorial, designed by Douglas W. Orr, was erected in 1959 as a "tribute to the honesty, indomitable courage, and high principles of free government symbolized by his life." The 10-ft- (3-m-) tall bronze statue, by American sculptor Wheeler Williams, is dwarfed by a 100-ft- (30-m-) high, white Tennessee marble bell tower (the Carillon) that rises up behind the figure of the politician.

6

Eastern Market

Q M8 **A** 7th & C Sts, SE **M** Eastern Market **O** 7am-7pm Tue-Fri, 7am-6pm Sat, 9am-5pm Sun **O** Jan 1, Jul 4, Thanksgiving, Dec 25 & 26 **w** easternmarket-dc.org

This block-long market hall has been a fixture in Capitol Hill since 1871, and the provisions sold today still have an Old World flavor. Big beef steaks and fresh pigs' feet are everywhere, along with gourmet sausages and cheeses from all over the world. The aroma of fresh bread, roasted chicken, and flowers pervades the hall. On Friday afternoons, Saturdays, and Sundays the covered stalls outside are filled with crafts and farmers' produce;

on Sundays these popular stalls also host a flea market. The market was designed by local architect Adolph Cluss. Destroyed in a fire in 2007, it has been rebuilt with modern interiors that retain their old charm. Along with Union Market north of the Capitol, it is one of the few public markets left in Washington that are still used for their original purpose.

EAT

Bistro Bis
Breakfast at this upscale French bistro is one of the best places in DC to spot celebrities and Congressional power brokers. Lunch and dinner are equally creative and rewarding.

Q K6 **A** 15 E St, NW **w** bistrobis.com

$$$

Thunder Grill
This Southwestern grill offers simple but delicious fare, with awe-inspiring views of Union Station.

Q L6 **A** 50 Massachusetts Ave, NE **w** thundergrilldc.com

$$$

7

US Botanic Garden

📍K8 🏛Independence Ave & 1st St, SW; entrance at 100 Maryland Ave, SW Ⓜ Federal Center SW 🕐10am–5pm daily 🌐usbg.gov

This stunningly beautiful conservatory and garden near the southwest corner of the Capitol is a wonderful oasis for families or anyone seeking a restful interlude from the hubbub of the Mall. The 80-ft-(24-m-) tall Palm House creates a spacious venue for a jungle of tropical and subtropical plants, including lush ferns and vibrantly colored orchids. Other specialties are plants native to deserts in the Old and New Worlds, plants of economic and healing value, and endangered plants rescued through an international trade program.

The Botanic Garden was originally established to cultivate plants that could be beneficial to the American people. It was revitalized in 1842, when the Wilkes Expedition to the South Seas brought back an assortment of plants from around the world, some of which are still on display.

A National Garden of plants native to the mid-Atlantic region was created on 3 acres (1 ha) of land west of the conservatory. It includes a Water Garden, a Rose Garden, and a terraced lawn. Visitors can dial (202) 730-9303 from their smartphones to stream an audio tour as they walk through the garden.

8

Bartholdi Park and Fountain

📍K8 🏛Independence Ave & 1st St, SW Ⓜ Federal Center SW 🕐Dawn–dusk daily 🌐usbg.gov/bartholdi-park

The graceful, symmetrical fountain that dominates this jewel of a park was created by Frédéric August Bartholdi (sculptor of the Statue of Liberty) for the Centennial Exposition of 1876, held in Philadelphia to mark the 100th anniversary of the signing of the Declaration of Independence. Originally lit by gas lamps, the Fountain of Light and Water was converted to electric lighting in 1881, becoming a popular nighttime attraction. Made of cast iron, it is decorated with figures of nymphs and tritons. Surrounding the fountain are tiny model gardens, planted to inspire the urban gardener. Themed areas in the park include therapeutic, romantic, and heritage plants, such as Virginia sneezeweed, Sweet William, and wild oats.

The stunning main reading room in the Library of Congress ↑

9

Library of Congress

📍L8 🏛101 Independence Ave, SE Ⓜ Capitol South 🕐8:30am–4.30pm Mon–Sat 🕐Jan 1, Thanksgiving, Dec 25 🌐loc.gov

This palatial edifice, built in Italian Renaissance style, is the hub of a network of stunning buildings that house the world's largest collection of books and other media. The library boasts an incredible 838 miles (1,349 km) of bookshelves that hold around 167 million items. Congress first established a reference library in the US Capitol in 1800. When the Capitol was burned down by the British in 1814, Jefferson sold his own collection to the government as a replacement, and his belief in a universality of knowledge became the foundation for the library's acquisition policy. Visitors can tour the legendary main reading room, with its 160-ft-(49-m-) high dome, and see collection items that include a 15th-century Gutenberg Bible.

←

Bartholdi Park, with its centerpiece fountain

⑫ Ebenezer United Methodist Church

📍 M9 🏛 4th & D Sts, SE
Ⓜ Eastern Market ⏰ 10am–2pm Tue–Fri 🔒 Federal hols

Established in 1827, this was the first black church to serve Methodists in Washington. Attendance grew rapidly, and a new church, Little Ebenezer, was built to take the overflow. After the 1863 Emancipation Proclamation, Congress ruled that black children should receive public education. In 1864, Little Ebenezer became DC's first school for black children. The number of members grew steadily and another church was built in 1868, but was damaged by a storm in 1896. The replacement, built in 1897, is Ebenezer United Methodist Church. A model of Little Ebenezer stands outside.

⑩ National Postal Museum

📍 L6 🏛 2 Massachusetts Ave, NE Ⓜ Union Station ⏰ 10am–5:30pm daily 🔒 Dec 25 🌐 postalmuseum.si.edu

Opened by the Smithsonian Institution in 1990, this fascinating museum is housed in the former City Post Office building. One of the centerpieces of the collection is the wood-and-fabric plane in which Sam Wiseman flew the first recorded airmail flight from Petaluma, California, to Santa Rosa in 1911. Other exhibits include a 1919 de Havilland DH4 biplane, which was the first official airmail service plane, along with a horse-drawn Concord Mail Coach and a postal rail car, showing how mail traveled before modern airmail.

The William H. Gross Stamp Gallery has one of the best stamp collections in the world. "Binding the Nation" explains the history of US mail to the end of the 19th century. Other exhibits illustrate how the mail system works and how a stamp is created. At postcard kiosks, you can address a postcard electronically, see the route it will take to its destination, and drop it in a mailbox on the spot.

---

⑪ Union Station

📍 L6 🏛 50 Massachusetts Ave, NE Ⓜ Union Station ⏰ 24 hours daily 🌐 unionstationdc.com

Spectacularly restored in 1988, the Beaux Arts Union Station offers visitors a potpourri of over 100 shops and restaurants, and a chance to stroll through one of the most dazzling architectural gems in the city.

When it was built in 1908, the elegantly proportioned white granite structure, its three main archways modeled on the Arch of Constantine in Rome, was the largest train station in the world. For half a century, it remained a major transportation hub, but as air travel became increasingly popular, passenger trains went into decline. Restoration work began in 1981, and included embellishing the 96-ft- (29-m-) high, barrel-vaulted ceiling with 22-carat gold leaf. Today, Union Station is visited by more than 40 million people a year.

A SHORT WALK
CAPITOL HILL

Distance 1.7 miles (2.7 km) **Nearest Metro** Capitol South
Time 35 minutes

The cityscape extending from the Capitol is an impressive combination of grand Classical architecture and stretches of grassy open spaces. There are no skyscrapers here, only the immense marble halls and columns that distinguish many of the government buildings. The bustle and excitement around the Capitol and Supreme Court contrast with the calm that can be found by the reflecting pool or in a quiet residential street. Many of the small touches that make the city special can be found in this area, such as the antique lighting fixtures on 2nd Street, the brilliant bursts of flowers along the sidewalks, or the brightly painted facades of the houses on 3rd Street near the Folger Shakespeare Library.

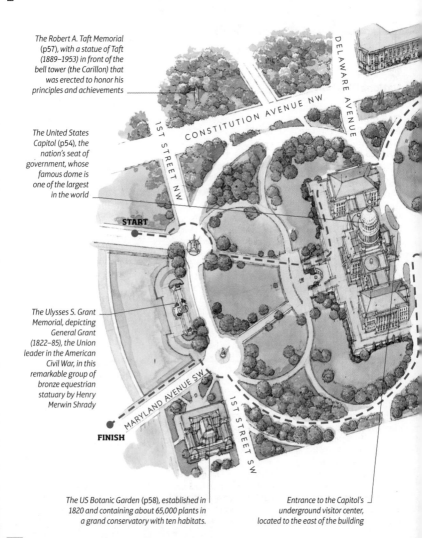

The Robert A. Taft Memorial (p57), with a statue of Taft (1889–1953) in front of the bell tower (the Carillon) that was erected to honor his principles and achievements

The United States Capitol (p54), the nation's seat of government, whose famous dome is one of the largest in the world

START

The Ulysses S. Grant Memorial, depicting General Grant (1822–85), the Union leader in the American Civil War, in this remarkable group of bronze equestrian statuary by Henry Merwin Shrady

FINISH

The US Botanic Garden (p58), established in 1820 and containing about 65,000 plants in a grand conservatory with ten habitats.

Entrance to the Capitol's underground visitor center, located to the east of the building

The beautifully decorated interiors of the Library of Congress

Locator Map
For more detail see p52

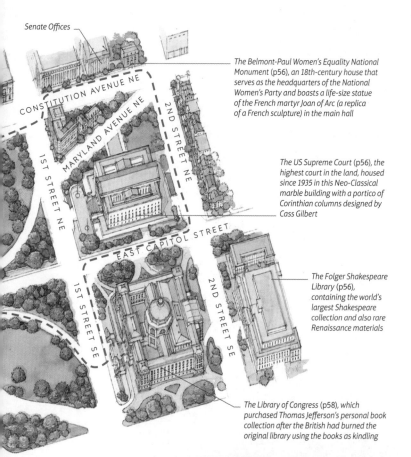

Senate Offices

The Belmont-Paul Women's Equality National Monument (p56), an 18th-century house that serves as the headquarters of the National Women's Party and boasts a life-size statue of the French martyr Joan of Arc (a replica of a French sculpture) in the main hall

The US Supreme Court (p56), the highest court in the land, housed since 1935 in this Neo-Classical marble building with a portico of Corinthian columns designed by Cass Gilbert

The Folger Shakespeare Library (p56), containing the world's largest Shakespeare collection and also rare Renaissance materials

The Library of Congress (p58), which purchased Thomas Jefferson's personal book collection after the British had burned the original library using the books as kindling

0 meters   150
0 yards   150

The Grant Memorial's Cavalry Group, showing soldiers riding onto the battlefield, about to crush their own comrade

I HAVE A DRE
MARTIN LUTHER KIN
THE MARCH ON WASHING
FOR JOBS AND FREEDO
AUGUST 28, 1963

THE MALL

In L'Enfant's original plan for the new capital of the United States, the Mall was conceived as a grand boulevard lined with diplomatic residences of elegant, Parisian-style architecture. L'Enfant's plan was never fully realized, but it is nevertheless a moving sight – this grand, tree-lined expanse is bordered on either side by the Smithsonian museums and features the Capitol at its eastern end and the Washington Monument at its western end. This dramatic formal version of the Mall did not materialize until after World War II. Until then the space was used for everything from a zoo to a railroad terminal to a wood yard. Today, the Mall forms a vital part of the history of the United States. Innumerable demonstrators have gathered at the Lincoln Memorial and marched to the US Capitol. The Pope said Mass, African-American soprano Marian Anderson sang at the request of first lady Eleanor Roosevelt, and Dr. Martin Luther King, Jr. delivered his famous "I Have a Dream" speech here. On summer evenings, teams of locals play softball and soccer on its fields, and every year, on the Fourth of July (Independence Day), America's birthday party is held on the Mall with a spectacular fireworks display.

D

E

F

PENNSYLVANIA AVE NW

LAFAYETTE
SQUARE

George Washington
University

White
House

VIRGINIA

F STREET NW

The Kennedy
Center

21ST STREET NW

AVENUE

STREET

NW

E STREET NW

The
Ellipse

NW

18TH STREET NW

17TH STREET NW

ELLIPSE ROAD NW

23RD STREET NW

7

ROCK CREEK AND POTOMAC PARKWAY NW

**WHITE HOUSE
AND FOGGY BOTTOM**
p104

CONSTITUTION   AVENUE   NW

HENRY BACON DR NW

14 Vietnam
Veterans Memorial

World War II
Memorial

17 Lincoln
Memorial

Reflecting Pool

12

Washington **13**
Monument

THE MALL

*Constitution
Gardens*

16 Korean War Veterans
Memorial

8

Arlington
Memorial
Bridge

INDEPENDENCE   AVENUE   SW

MAINE AVE SW

*West
Potomac
Park*

WEST BASIN DRIVE SW

15 Martin Luther
King, Jr. Memorial

Kutz
Bridge

OHIO

P o t o m a c

20
Tidal Basin

Tidal Basin
Boathouse

DRIVE

18 Franklin D. Roosevelt
Memorial

R i v e r

SW

Jefferson
Memorial
19

9

GEORGE WASHINGTON MEMORIAL PARKWAY

George Mason
Memorial Garden

OHIO DRIVE SW

George Mason
Memorial Bridge

Arland D Williams
Memorial Bridge

395

10

THE MALL

D

E

F

THE MALL

Must Sees

1. National Gallery of Art
2. National Air and Space Museum
3. National Museum of Natural History
4. National Museum of American History
5. National Museum of African American History and Culture

Experience More

6. National Museum of the American Indian
7. Smithsonian Castle
8. Arthur M. Sackler Gallery
9. Hirshhorn Museum
10. National Museum of African Art
11. Freer Gallery of Art
12. World War II Memorial
13. Washington Monument
14. Vietnam Veterans Memorial
15. Martin Luther King, Jr. Memorial
16. Korean War Veterans Memorial
17. Lincoln Memorial
18. Franklin D. Roosevelt Memorial
19. Jefferson Memorial
20. Tidal Basin

Eat

1. Sweet Home Café
2. America's Table
3. Mitsitam Café
4. Pavilion Café
5. Castle Café

❶ Ⓜ 🍴 🖥 🛍

NATIONAL GALLERY OF ART

📍J7 🚇Between 3rd & 9th Sts & Constitution Ave, NW on the Mall Ⓜ Archives-Navy Memorial-Penn Quarter, Judiciary Square, Smithsonian 🚌32, 34, 36, 70 🕐10am-5pm Mon-Sat, 11am-6pm Sun 🚫Jan 1, Dec 25 💻nga.gov

Housing one of the world's great collections of art, the National Gallery is itself an architectural masterpiece, and boasts a collection that includes over 150,000 paintings, prints, sculptures, and virtually every other type of artwork imaginable.

The gallery's two buildings are an unusual pair. The beautiful West Building is a majestic Neo-Classical structure designed by John Russell Pope. Opened in 1941, it displays the core of the museum's collection. The airy East Building, a radically angular counterpoint built by famed architect I. M. Pei in 1978, is a huge, fluid space, with galleries on either side holding works by modern and contemporary artists. Its lofty atrium is dominated by Alexander Calder's last and largest work, a huge mobile designed especially for the space. The open, green, and delightful Sculpture Garden lies next to the West Building.

ANDREW MELLON

In the 1920s, American financier and statesman Andrew Mellon began traveling the world and collecting art, including works from Russia's Hermitage. He offered his collection to the country in 1936, along with the funds to build a national gallery.

126

paintings and 26 statues gifted by Andrew Mellon formed the gallery's initial collection.

1 The well-known biblical story of Daniel is depicted in the powerful *Daniel in the Lion's Den* by Peter Paul Rubens (c 1614–1616), one of the 17th century's greatest masters.

2 Despite its light palette and tranquil atmosphere, Edward Hopper's 1939 *Ground Swell* reflects leitmotifs of loneliness and escape that were typical of the artist's works.

3 A large, dramatic triangular atrium is the focus of the trapezoidal East Building, which was completed in 1978.

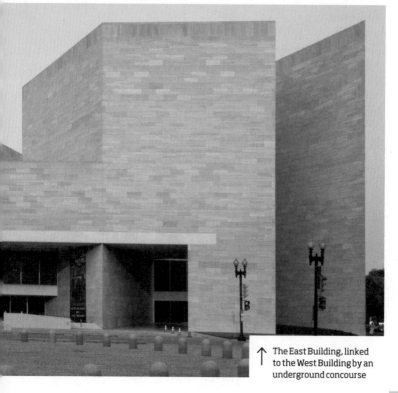

↑ The East Building, linked to the West Building by an underground concourse

Exploring the National Gallery of Art

The West Building holds the majority of the collection, with significant exhibits of Byzantine and Renaissance art, as well as a dazzling array of Impressionist works by Monet, Van Gogh, Cassatt, and Renoir, among others. Pei's H-shaped East Building is home to modern and contemporary works. Renovations added 12,250 sq ft (1,138 sq m), making room for important works by Pablo Picasso, Mark Rothko, Alexander Calder, Barbara Kruger, and other artists. The Sculpture Garden features works by artists such as Calder, Marc Chagall, and Tony Smith.

↑ Works by Rothko in the National Gallery's modern art collections

Did You Know?

Da Vinci's *Ginevra de' Benci* is displayed as a walk-around, as both sides of the work are painted.

Calder's mobile *Untitled* (1976), on display in the East Building atrium ↑

Top Collections

13th- to 16th-century Italian Art

The collection features art that illustrates the transition from the Byzantine influence to the more expressive and realistic Renaissance style. Highlights include Pietro Perugino's *The Crucifixion with the Virgin, St. John, St. Jerome and St. Mary Magdalene*, Raphael's *The Alba Madonna* (1510), called by one writer "the supreme compositional achievement of Renaissance painting," and Fra Angelico and Fra Filippo Lippi's *Adoration of the Magi* (c 1440/1460) *(right)*.

16th-century Italian, Spanish, and French Art

The 1500s were the height of Italian Classicism. *Christ at the Sea of Galilee* (c 1575/1580) by Venetian master Jacopo Tintoretto typifies the style. The emotionally intense painting portrays Christ standing on the shore. There are also works by Titian and Raphael.

17th- to 18th-century Italian, Spanish, and French Art

Among these works are El Greco's *Christ Cleansing the Temple* (pre-1570), which demonstrates 16th-century Italian influence. El Greco ("The Greek") signed his real name, Domenikos Theotokopoulos, to the panel.

17th-century Dutch and Flemish Art

This collection holds a number of Old Masters including works by Van Dyck, Rubens, Vermeer, and Rembrandt. *Girl With a Red Hat* (c 1666) by Johannes Vermeer is a masterpiece demonstrating the artist's virtuosity in harmonizing light with brilliant color.

19th-century French Art

One of the best Impressionist collections outside Paris, this includes Claude Monet's *The Bridge at Argenteuil* (1874) *(left)*. Post-Impressionist works include Toulouse-Lautrec's *Quadrille at the Moulin Rouge* (1892), depicting a dancer.

American Art

An important collection, this shows European influence, but in themes that are resolutely American. Examples include James McNeill Whistler's *Mother of Pearl and Silver: The Andalusian* (1888-1900) and *Breezing Up (A Fair Wind)* (1873-6), a masterpiece by the American Realist Winslow Homer.

Modern and Contemporary Art

The collection includes *Untitled* (1976), a vast mobile by Alexander Calder, Henry Moore's bronze sculpture *Knife Edge Mirror Two Piece* (1977-8), and works by Lichtenstein, Pollock, Rothko, and others.

Sculpture Garden

The elegant Sculpture Garden showcases 17 sculptures, including pieces by Louise Bourgeois and Joan Miró. Transformed into an ice rink in winter and a concert venue in summer, the garden functions both as an outdoor gallery and as a pleasant oasis within the city.

2 🏛 🍴 🖵 🛍

NATIONAL AIR AND SPACE MUSEUM

📍 J8 🏠 The Mall, Independence Ave at 6th St, SW Ⓜ Smithsonian 🚌 32, 34, 36, 52
🕐 10am–5:30pm daily 🌐 airandspace.si.edu

At its core, this museum celebrates the most fundamental of human dreams: the longing to break the bonds of earth, to fly, and reach for the stars. In its lofty, light-filled galleries, scores of famous planes hang overhead, while the floor is filled with rockets, spacecraft, and artifacts tracing the story of flight.

A great place for all enthusiasts of flight, the remarkable National Air and Space Museum attracts over seven million visitors every year. Reflecting the idea of flight, the soaring architecture of the 1976 building complements the thousands of exhibits on display within. The museum serves up a mind-bending array of sights and experiences, geared for all ages, that fire the imagination. Here visitors can learn about the origins of flight, admire some of the world's most storied air- and spacecraft, and discover the long road of innovation, failure, and success that led humans from wood and fabric wings to Mars landings.

GALLERY GUIDE

Both floors house themed displays. The first floor has a public observatory and a food court; the second has the Lockheed Martin IMAX® Theater and the Einstein Planetarium. Aircraft and spacecraft are suspended from the lofty ceilings.

↑ The red Lockheed Vega of Amelia Earhart, the first woman to make a solo transatlantic flight

Timeline

1894

△ The graceful Lilienthal Glider developed by German aeronautical pioneer Otto Lilienthal lays the foundation for the Wright Brothers' flight experiments.

1928

△ The largest commercial plane in existence when introduced in 1926, the Ford Tri-Motor becomes known as "The Tin Goose."

1947

△ Made famous in the movie *The Right Stuff*, the Bell X-1 is the plane in which legendary pilot Chuck Yeager breaks the sound barrier in 1947.

1970

△ The Lunar Module LM-2 shuttles two astronauts from the Command Module orbiting the moon to the surface and back.

↑ The "America by Air" exhibit, outlining the history and global effect of the US airline industry

Exploring the National Air and Space Museum

There is a wealth of legendary planes and spacecraft here, like the Wright Flyer and the *Spirit of St. Louis*. But tucked away are also many lesser-known treats, like John Glenn's space suit and a Fokker T-2 that made the first nonstop US transcontinental flight in 1923. Exhibits such as "America by Air," "Space Race," and "Apollo to the Moon" highlight unique chapters in flight and space exploration, while interactive displays allow visitors to touch a real moon rock, walk through the Skylab space station, or use a flight simulator to fly a fighter jet.

↑ The *Spirit of St. Louis*, in which the 25-year-old Charles Lindbergh made the first solo transatlantic flight in May 1927

 HIDDEN GEM
Flight Simulators

Flight simulators offer virtual reality, capsule simulations, and traditional flight. For a fee, these give visitors experiences that range from flying a World War I triplane to taking an exciting space walk.

←

The historic Mercury *Friendship* 7 capsule, in which astronaut John Glenn became the first American to orbit the earth in 1961

> INSIDER TIP
> **Tours for Trekkies**
>
> To celebrate the infinite diversity among its visitors, the museum – which says it is one of the galaxy's most popular attractions – offers an audio tour in Klingon via its smartphone app.

1 The soaring "Boeing Milestones of Flight" gallery highlights major firsts in aviation and space travel, including the groundbreaking SpaceShipOne.

2 One of the museum's most popular artifacts is the touchable moon rock in the "Boeing Milestones of Flight" exhibit.

3 Artifacts in the "Space Race" gallery, including John Glenn's space suit, trace the breakneck rivalry between the US and USSR from 1957 to 1975.

Did You Know?

Overall this huge museum covers an area equivalent to the size of 18 football fields.

The rotunda's massive African bush elephant, one of the highlights of the museum ↑

Geology, Gems & Minerals

3 Ⓜ 🖵 🛍

NATIONAL MUSEUM OF NATURAL HISTORY

📍H7 🏛Constitution Ave & 10th St, NW Ⓜ Smithsonian, Federal Triangle 🚌32, 34, 36
🕐10am-5:30pm daily 🌐mnh.si.edu

Dedicated to inspiring curiosity and discovery about our natural world, from ancient life forms and our earliest ancestors to the diverse cultures of today, the National Museum of Natural History has plenty to fascinate all ages, making this one of the most popular museums on the Mall, with seven million annual visitors.

The museum, which opened in 1910, preserves cultural and historical artifacts and collects samples of fossils and living creatures from land and sea. Visiting the museum is a vast undertaking, so sample the best of the exhibits and leave the rest for return visits. The Live Insect Zoo explores the lives and habitats of earth's single largest animal group and, with its giant hissing cockroaches and leaf-cutter ant colony, is popular with children, while the Dinosaur Hall delights young and old alike. The stunning Hall of Mammals has 274 specimens, and looks at how they adapted to changes in habitat and climate over millions of years.

↑ The museum's simple, Neo-Classical exterior

↑ Marine specimens, high-definition videos, and the latest technology at the Sant Ocean Hall, allowing exploration of the ocean's past, present, and future

↑ The Hall of Mammals, filled with dramatic represen-tations explaining the diversity of mammals

GALLERY GUIDE

The first floor's main exhibitions include human origins, mammals, and marine life. Dinosaurs and mummies are on the second level, alongside the Gems and Minerals collection, the Live Insect Zoo, and the Live Butterfly Pavilion. Tweens and teens will enjoy Q?rius, an interactive learning space on the ground and first floors.

4 ⓧ 🍴 🖥 🛍

NATIONAL MUSEUM OF AMERICAN HISTORY

📍 G7 🚪 Between 12th & 14th Sts, NW & Constitution Ave Ⓜ Smithsonian, Federal Triangle 🚌 32, 34, 36 🕐 10am–5:30pm daily 🌐 americanhistory.si.edu

This charming museum is filled with interesting artifacts from America's past. From a Colonial gunboat and Lincoln's hat to Kermit the Frog and Dorothy's ruby slippers, the objects cover unique moments and cultural touchstones in American history.

The museum has a flair for gathering its fascinating artifacts into powerful and informative exhibits. From the American Revolution to the space race, displays follow the nation's journey from its origins to its future. "America on the Move" tells the story of a mobile nation, while "Within These Walls" illustrates America's history through a real house that once stood in Massachusetts and the stories of five families that occupied it over 200 years. This is also a great museum for children, with lots of interactive displays, artifacts with wow-power, and instantly recognizable pieces like the Star-Spangled Banner and Mr. Roger's red sweater.

Did You Know?

About 8 ft (2.5 m) of the Star-Spangled Banner is missing as over the years people took pieces as souvenirs.

GALLERY GUIDE

The first floor features science and transportation exhibits alongside Spark!Lab. The next floor has the Star-Spangled Banner and the groundbreaking exhibition, "The Nation We Build Together", which questions American ideas of religion, diversity, and democracy. The third floor offers an eclectic selection including the "First Ladies" exhibit and the gunboat *Philadelphia*.

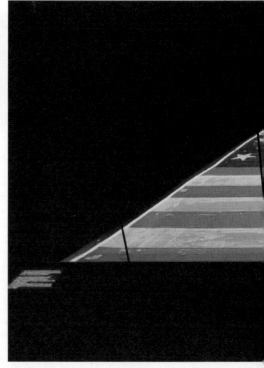

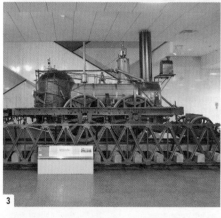

1 Spark!Lab invites kids to participate in entertaining science experiments in a supervised environment.

2 The rough, open wooden gunboat *Philadelphia* was sunk in 1776 while defending Lake Champlain, whose cold waters preserved it until its recovery and restoration in 1935.

3 The oldest operable locomotive in the world, the 1831 wood and steel *John Bull*, named for a fictional English gentleman, ran between New York City and Philadelphia.

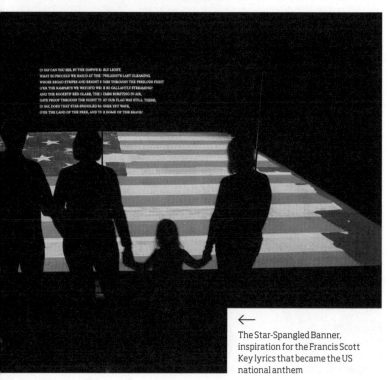

← The Star-Spangled Banner, inspiration for the Francis Scott Key lyrics that became the US national anthem

5 🖥 🏛

NATIONAL MUSEUM OF AFRICAN AMERICAN HISTORY AND CULTURE

📍 G7 🏠 1400 Constitution Ave, NW Ⓜ Smithsonian 🚌 13, 52 🕙 10am–5:30pm daily
🌐 nmaahc.si.edu

This powerful museum traces African-American history from the roots of slavery to the election of an African-American president and beyond. The galleries begin 70 ft (21 m) underground with exhibits on slavery and segregation, rising to higher, brighter floors that focus on emancipation and civil rights, and offer an inspirational look at a people striving to take their rightful place in the nation.

The museum's collections are designed to support three pillars of the African-American story: History, Culture, and Community. These are told through ten major exhibit galleries. In addition to slavery and segregation, these halls highlight African-American contributions to sports, music, visual arts, and military history. "Hometown Hub" examines ten geographical centers of unique African-American experience, such as Chicago and South Carolina. The museum also houses a 350-seat theater and the award-winning Sweet Home Café. The museum is so popular that timed entry passes are needed. Advance and a few same-day passes are available online, and a limited number of walk-up passes are also offered after 1pm on weekdays.

100,000

slaves were helped to escape by the Underground Railroad, but that was only 2 percent of those enslaved.

1 "Musical Crossroads" tells the story of African-American music from the arrival of the first Africans to the present.

2 The Serenity Room is a space to meditate on the thought-provoking themes and exhibits.

3 The striking building is covered in 3,600 bronze-colored cast aluminum panels that form a lattice, symbolizing upward striving.

Must See

Exhibit depicting the →
1968 Olympics human
rights salute by Tommie
Smith and John Carlos

Timeline

Before 1864	*1876–1968*	*1955–1968*	*2009*
▲ The Underground Railroad leads slaves to freedom, and Harriet Tubman (1822-1913) is one of its most successful "conductors."	▲ Defying the prevailing segregation laws, four African-Americans occupy these stools at a Woolworths store on February 1, 1960.	▲ America's Civil Rights movement effectively ends segregation and improves the lives of millions of African-Americans.	▲ The Obama White House marks the participation of African-Americans at the very highest levels of US government.

EXPERIENCE MORE

6

National Museum of the American Indian

📍J8 🏛The Mall, 4th St & Independence Ave, SW Ⓜ L'Enfant Plaza 🕙10am–5:30pm daily 🌐americanindian.si.edu

Anyone who has ever been fascinated by the history or culture of Native Americans will want to visit this elegant museum. With its sweeping natural curves reminiscent of the red-rock country of the American Southwest, the building is set in a landscape of flowing water, hardwood forest, meadowland, and croplands to reflect the American Indian connection to the land.

Established in collaboration with the Native American communities throughout the western hemisphere, this is the only national museum dedicated to Native peoples. The exhibits showcase the spiritual and daily lives of diverse peoples and encourage visitors to look beyond stereotypes. "Many Hands, Many Voices" features more than 3,500 objects, including beaded objects and artwork, and is a good place to start. Even more impressive are the exhibits that offer a first-hand look into the life and beliefs of numerous indigenous cultures. In "Nation to Nation," American Indians tell their own stories and histories via artifacts and videos, focusing on both the destruction of their culture and on their resilience. In "Our Universes," eight groups of Native peoples share their world views, creation philosophies, and relationship with nature.

JAMES SMITHSON

Although he never visited the United States, English philanthropist James Smithson (1765–1829) left his fortune to "found at Washington [...] an establishment for the increase and diffusion of knowledge among men." Congress used his bequest to set up a foundation to administer all national museums, and the first Smithson collection was shown at the Smithsonian Castle in 1855.

JAMES SMITHSON

7

Smithsonian Castle

📍H8 🏛1000 Jefferson Dr, SW Ⓜ Smithsonian 🕙8:30am–5:30pm daily 🌐si.edu

Constructed of red sandstone in 1855, the ornate, Victorian Smithsonian Castle served as the first home of the Smithsonian Institution, and today houses its information center and administrative offices. The South Tower Room was the first children's room in a Washington

museum. Outside the castle is the rose garden, filled with beautiful hybrid tea roses.

↑ One of the pair of bronze *Lions of Timna* at the Sackler Gallery

---

Arthur M. Sackler Gallery

⬤H8 🏛1050 Independence Ave, SW Ⓜ Smithsonian ⏰10am–5:30pm daily 🌐asia.si.edu

Dr. Arthur M. Sackler, a New York physician, started collecting Asian art in the 1950s. In 1982, he donated more than 1,000 artifacts, along with $4 million in funds, to the Smithsonian Institution to establish this museum.

The Sackler's 3,000-piece collection is particularly rich in Chinese works, and highlights

include a stunning display of Chinese bronzes and jades, some dating back to 4000 BC. There are also 7th-century Ming ceramics and an extensive range of sculpture from India and Southeast Asia.

In 1987 the gallery acquired the impressive Vever Collection, which includes Islamic books from the 11th to the 19th centuries, 19th- and 20th-century Japanese prints, Japanese, Chinese, and Indian paintings, and modern photography.

Hirshhorn Museum

⬤H8 🏛Independence Ave & 7th St, SW Ⓜ L'Enfant Plaza ⏰Museum: 10am–5:30pm daily; sculpture garden: 7:30am–dusk) 🌐hirshhorn.si.edu

The Hirshhorn's building has been variously described as a doughnut or a flying saucer, but it is actually a four-story, not-quite-symmetrical cylinder. It is home to one of the greatest collections of modern art in the United States.

The museum's benefactor, Joseph H. Hirshhorn, was an eccentric, flamboyant Latvian immigrant who amassed

6,000 pieces of contemporary art; the collection now has double that number. The main floor displays newly acquired work, while the second floor hosts temporary exhibitions. The third floor houses the permanent collection, which includes works by artists such as Alexander Calder, Arshile Gorky, Willem de Kooning, and John Singer Sargent. The sculpture garden outside includes pieces by Calder, Rodin, and Matisse.

National Museum of African Art

⬤H8 🏛950 Independence Ave, SW Ⓜ Smithsonian ⏰10am–5:30pm daily 🌐africa.si.edu

This is the first US museum to concentrate solely on the art and culture of the African continent. The underground galleries are accessed through an entrance pavilion in the Enid A. Haupt Garden, in front of the Smithsonian Castle.

Visitors can explore three subterranean floors that hold the museum's 9,000-piece permanent collection, which includes both modern and ancient art from Africa. Traditional art in gold, bronze, and ceramic is on display, along with an extensive collection of masks. There is also a display of brightly colored, patterned *kente* cloth from Ghana, often used for special occasions and as a symbol of African nationalism. The Eliot Elisofon Photographic Archives (Eliot Elisofon was a famous photographer for *Life* magazine) contain 300,000 prints and some 120,000 ft (36,576 m) of film footage on African art and culture.

The museum hosts dance, music, and spoken word events. There is also a full calendar of educational tours, lectures, and workshops, including many for children.

INSIDER TIP
Smithsonian Carousel

Kids and adults love the 1947 carousel set near the Smithsonian Castle. As well as its traditional music and ornately carved horses, there's also a popular sea dragon to ride.

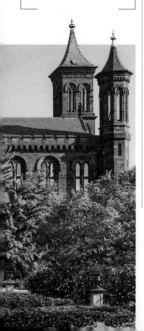

← The Smithsonian Castle, built in imposing Gothic Revival style

11 🛍

Freer Gallery of Art

📍H8 🏛Jefferson Dr & 12th
St, SW Ⓜ Smithsonian
🕐10am–5:30pm daily
🌐asia.si.edu

Named after Charles Lang
Freer, a railroad magnate
who donated his collection of
9,000 pieces of American and
Asian art to the Smithsonian,
the Freer Gallery opened in
1923, becoming the first
Smithsonian museum of art.
Constructed in the Italian
Renaissance style, the Freer
has an attractive courtyard
with a fountain at its center.
There are 19 galleries, most
with skylights that illuminate
a superb collection of Asian
and American art. In the Asian
Art collection are examples
of Chinese, Japanese, and
Korean art, including sculpture, ceramics, paintings, and
folding screens. The gallery
also has a fine selection of
Buddhist sculpture, as well
as paintings and calligraphy
from India.

There is also a select
collection of American art.
The most astonishing work is
James McNeill Whistler's "The
Peacock Room." Whistler
painted a dining room for
British shipowner Frederick
Leyland in London, who
found that it was not to his
taste. Freer purchased the
room in 1904 and had it
dismantled and moved to
Washington. In contrast
to the subtle ele-
gance of the other
rooms in the
gallery, this one
is a riot of blues,
greens, and golds,
with Whistler's gor-
geously painted
peacocks covering
the walls and ceiling.

→

A 12th-13th-century
Chinese Bodhisattva
statue at the Freer
Gallery of Art

The imposing granite pillars
of Washington's national
World War II Memorial ↑

12

World War II Memorial

📍F8 🏛17th St, NW
between Constitution
& Independence Aves
Ⓜ Smithsonian, Federal
Triangle 🕐24 hrs daily
🌐nps.gov/nwwm

Sixteen million Americans
served in World War II, and
of those, 400,000 died. The
4,000 gold stars – the Field of
Stars –on the Freedom Wall
commemorate these war
dead. Millions more ordinary
citizens contributed to the
war effort. The World
War II Memorial honors
their service and sacri-
fice. Its dedication
ceremony on May
29, 2004 attracted
150,000 people,
many of them
veterans. The
monument
features a 43-ft-
(13-m-) long
pavilion on
each side of the
Rainbow Pool
to represent the
Atlantic and Pacific
theaters of war. Fifty-
six granite pillars
stand for each of the
country's states and

territories during that time.
Bas-relief panels by sculptor
Ray Kaskey line both sides of
the 17th Street entrance. They
depict the many contributions
Americans made to the war
effort: from enlistment and
embarkation to medics in the
field and Rosie the Riveter
(symbolizing the help given
by American women).

Words spoken by generals
and presidents are inscribed
throughout the memorial,
including these by General
Douglas MacArthur marking
the war's end: "Today the guns
are silent… The skies no
longer rain death – the seas
bear only commerce – men
everywhere walk upright in
the sunlight. The entire world
is quietly at peace."

> 💬 INSIDER TIP
> **Find Kilroy!**
>
> At the World War II
> Memorial, kids can have
> a great time hunting for
> the two iconic "Kilroy
> Was Here" images that
> are carved into the
> stone, similar to the
> ones that American GIs
> drew everywhere
> during the war.

EAT

Sweet Home Café

Down-home Southern, creole, northern, and western dishes reflect the African-American culinary experience.

 G7 1400 Constitution Ave, NW W nmaahc.si.edu

$$$

America's Table

Classic American fare, including hamburgers, barbecue, and Tex-Mex.

 G7 1300 Constitution Ave, NW W americanhistory. si.edu

$$$

Mitsitam Café

Creative meals based on the traditional foods of indigenous peoples, from bison burgers to grilled salmon.

 J8 4th Ave, SW W americanindian. si.edu

$$$

Pavilion Café

Charming café with a patio overlooking the National Gallery's Sculpture Garden.

 H7 7th St & Constitution Ave, NW W pavilioncafe.com

$$$

Castle Café

This soup-and-sandwich bistro is the perfect choice for a quick lunch.

 H8 1000 Jefferson Dr, SW W si.edu/dining

$$$

Washington Monument

G8 Independence Ave at 17th St, SW M Smithsonian 9am-5pm daily (Memorial Day-Labor Day: to 10pm) W nps. gov/wamo

Made from 36,000 pieces of marble and granite, this tribute to the first US president is one of the city's most recognizable sights. Funds initially came from individual citizens, and building began in 1848. When the money ran out, the work stopped for 25 years. Then, in 1876, President Ulysses S. Grant authorized the project's completion. A slight change in the color of stone shows where construction resumed.

Vietnam Veterans Memorial

E7 22nd St & Constitution Ave, NW M Smithsonian 24 hrs daily W nps.gov/vive

Maya Lin, a 21-year-old student at Yale University, submitted a design for the proposed Vietnam Veterans Memorial as part of her architecture course. One of 1,421 entries, Maya Lin's design was simple – two triangular black walls sinking into the earth at an angle of 125 degrees, one end pointing to the Lincoln Memorial, the other to the Washington Monument. On the walls would be inscribed the names, in chronological order, of the more than 58,000 Americans who died in the Vietnam War, from the first death in 1959 to the last in 1975. Since the names are not in alphabetical order, there is a book listing all the names that correspond to a panel.

Lin received only a B grade on her university course, but she won the competition to design the memorial. It has become one of the most moving monuments on the Mall. Veterans and their families leave tokens of remembrance – soft toys, poems, pictures, and bunches of flowers – at the site of their fallen soldier's name.

Nearby, an evocative statue of three soldiers awaiting airlift, sculpted by Frederick Hart, was added in 1984, and the Vietnam Women's Memorial was built in 1993.

↑ The striking figures of the Korean War Veterans Memorial

Martin Luther King, Jr. Memorial

📍 F8 🏠 1850 West Basin Dr, SW Ⓜ Smithsonian, Foggy Bottom-GWU ⏰ 24 hrs daily 🌐 nps.gov/mlkm

Set among the famous cherry blossom trees of the Tidal Basin is the Mall's first memorial to an African-American. Dedicated on August 26, 2011, it commemorates the life and work of Dr. King. Designed by Chinese sculptor Lei Yixin, the memorial consists of two huge stone tablets – one features excerpts from King's speeches, while the other shows his figure emerging from the stone. The choice of a non-American sculptor proved highly controversial, as did King's somewhat stern expression.

Korean War Veterans Memorial

📍 E8 🏠 10 Daniel French Dr, SW Ⓜ Smithsonian, Foggy Bottom-GWU ⏰ 24 hrs daily 🌐 nps.gov/kwvm

The Korean War Veterans Memorial is a controversial tribute to a controversial war. Although 1.5 million Americans served in the conflict, war was never officially declared and it is often known as "The Forgotten War." Intense debate preceded the selection of the memorial's design. On July 27, 1995, on the 42nd anniversary of the armistice that ended the war, the memorial was dedicated. Nineteen larger-than-life stainless steel statues, a squad on patrol, are shown moving toward the American flag as their symbolic objective. The ponchos they wear are a reminder of the war's notoriously miserable weather conditions. On the south side of the memorial is a polished black granite wall etched with the images of more than 2,400 veterans.

An inscription above the Pool of Remembrance reads: "Our nation honors her sons and daughters who answered the call to defend a country they never knew and a people they never met."

Lincoln Memorial

📍 E8 🏠 Constitution Ave between French & Bacon Dr Ⓜ Smithsonian, Foggy Bottom-GWU, then 20-min walk ⏰ 24 hrs daily (some areas may be closed in 2019 due to renovation work; check the website for details) 🌐 nps.gov/linc

One of the least promising proposals for a memorial to President Lincoln was for a monument on swampy land to the west of the Washington Monument. Yet this was to become one of the city's most awe-inspiring sights. Looming over the Reflecting Pool is the huge seated figure of Lincoln in his Neo-Classical "temple" with 36 Doric columns, one for each state at the time of his death. Today, it is a national touchstone for socially progressive movements. It is an icon of the Civil Rights movement, and it was from its steps in 1963 that Dr. King gave his "I Have a Dream" speech. Inside, engraved on the south wall is the Gettysburg Address (p186). Above it is a mural by Jules Guerin depicting the angel of truth freeing a slave.

18

Franklin D. Roosevelt Memorial

🔲 F9 🏛 400 W Basin Dr, SW
Ⓜ Smithsonian, then 25-min walk ⏲ 24 hrs daily
🌐 nps.gov/fdrm

Franklin D. Roosevelt once told Supreme Court Justice Felix Frankfurter, "If they are to put up any memorial to me… I should like it to consist of a block about the size of this," pointing to his desk.

It took more than 50 years for a fitting monument to be built, but Roosevelt's plea for modesty was not heeded. Opened in 1997, this memorial is a huge park of four granite open-air rooms, one for each of Roosevelt's terms. The first room has a bronze bas-relief. In the second room, *Breadline* by George Segal recalls the Great Depression, during which Roosevelt was re-elected three times. Neil Estern's sculpture in the third room portrays the president, a polio sufferer, sitting in a wheelchair hidden by his Navy cape, with his beloved little terrier Fala by his side. In the last room, waterfalls cascade down into a series of pools, whose waters reflect the peace that Roosevelt was so keen to achieve before his death.

HISTORY OF THE MALL

In 1789, Frenchman Pierre L'Enfant (1754–1825), the city's first town planner, envisioned a grand avenue running west from the Capitol, but years later the area remained swampy and undeveloped. It wasn't until the end of the Civil War, in 1865, that Lincoln ordered work to begin again, and the Mall began to take on the park-like appearance it has today. The addition of museums and memorials in the 20th century confirmed the Mall as Washington's cultural heart and "America's Front Yard."

19

Jefferson Memorial

🔲 G9 🏛 South bank of the Tidal Basin Ⓜ Smithsonian
⏲ 24 hrs daily 🌐 nps.gov/thje

Thomas Jefferson (*p188*) was a political philosopher, architect, musician, book collector, scientist, horticulturist, diplomat, inventor, and the third American president, from 1801 to 1809. He also played a significant part in drafting the Declaration of Independence. The memorial was suggested by Franklin D. Roosevelt, who felt that Jefferson's contribution was as important as Lincoln's for the history of the US. Designed by John Russell Pope, this Neo-Classical memorial was dedicated in 1943 and holds a 19-ft- (6-m-) tall bronze of Jefferson.

20

Tidal Basin

🔲 F9 🏛 Boathouse: 1501 Maine Ave, SW
Ⓜ Smithsonian

The Tidal Basin was built in 1897 to catch the Potomac's overflow and prevent flooding. In 1912, cherry trees, a gift of the Japanese government, were planted along the shores of the man-made lake. During the two weeks when the trees bloom (mid-March to mid-April) the area teems with visitors who come to walk under canopies of gracefully arching branches laden with pink blossoms, picnic on the lawns, or go paddleboating in the Tidal Basin.

↓ Cherry trees framing the Jefferson Memorial

A SHORT WALK
THE MALL

Distance 1.5 miles (2.5 km) **Nearest Metro** Smithsonian
Time 30 minutes

This 1 mile (1.5 km) boulevard between the Capitol and the Washington Monument is the city's cultural heart, with the many different museums of the Smithsonian Institution set along this green strip. At the northeast corner of the Mall is the National Gallery of Art and its pleasant Sculpture Garden. Standing directly opposite the gallery is one of the most popular museums in the world – the National Air and Space Museum, a vast, soaring construction of steel and glass. Both the National Museum of American History and the National Museum of Natural History, on the north side of the Mall, also draw huge numbers of visitors.

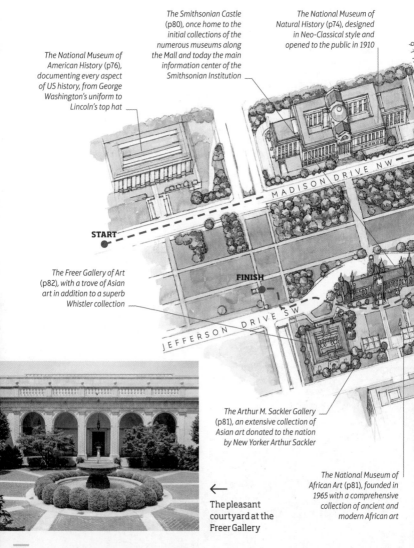

The Smithsonian Castle (p80), once home to the initial collections of the numerous museums along the Mall and today the main information center of the Smithsonian Institution

The National Museum of Natural History (p74), designed in Neo-Classical style and opened to the public in 1910

The National Museum of American History (p76), documenting every aspect of US history, from George Washington's uniform to Lincoln's top hat

9TH ST

MADISON DRIVE NW

START

The Freer Gallery of Art (p82), with a trove of Asian art in addition to a superb Whistler collection

FINISH

JEFFERSON DRIVE SW

The Arthur M. Sackler Gallery (p81), an extensive collection of Asian art donated to the nation by New Yorker Arthur Sackler

The National Museum of African Art (p81), founded in 1965 with a comprehensive collection of ancient and modern African art

← The pleasant courtyard at the Freer Gallery

The superb National Gallery of Art (p66), with paintings and other works of art that chronicle the history of art from the Middle Ages to the 20th century

Locator Map
For more detail see p64

National Gallery of Art, West Building

National Gallery of Art, Sculpture Garden

CONSTITUTION AVENUE NW

7TH STREET NW

National Gallery of Art, East Building

MADISON DRIVE NW

7TH STREET NW

The National Air and Space Museum (p70), with its clean, modern design echoing the technological advances in aviation illustrated by the spectacular exhibits inside

INDEPENDENCE AVENUE SW

0 meters 100
0 yards 100

N ↑

The Hirshhorn Museum (p81), with an unusual cylindrical building housing a collection of 18,000 pieces of contemporary art

The Arts and Industries Building, a masterpiece of Victorian architecture originally built to contain exhibits from the 1876 Centennial Exposition in Philadelphia

↑ Barbara Kruger's *Belief+Doubt* installation at the Hirshhorn

PENN QUARTER

Bordered by the Capitol to the east and the White House to the west, Washington's Penn Quarter was the heart of the city at the start of the 20th century. F Street, the city's first paved road, bustled with shops, bars, newspaper offices, and churches, as well as horses and carriages. Penn Quarter was also an important residential neighborhood. The upper classes kept elegant homes, while middle-class merchants lived above their shops. By the 1950s suburbia had lured people away, and in the 1980s Penn Quarter was a mixture of boarded-up buildings and discount shops. The 1990s saw a dramatic change and the beginnings of regeneration, as the Capital One Arena attracted trendy new eateries and upscale brands. Today, Washington's city center continues to flourish as a thriving hub of activity, filled with shops, hotels, restaurants, and theaters.

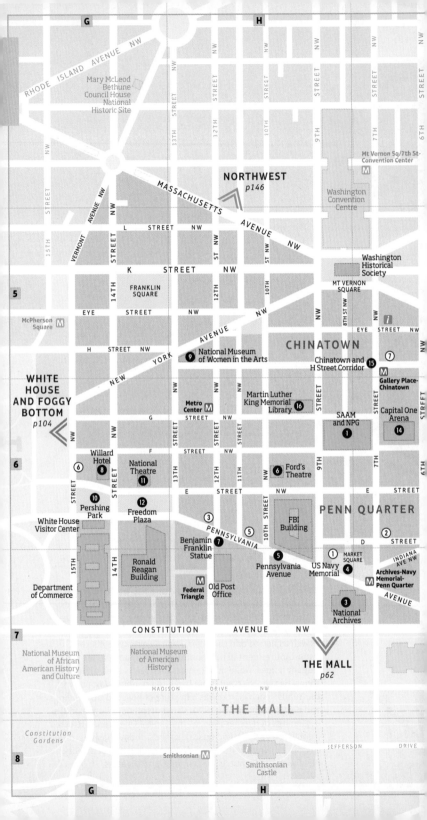

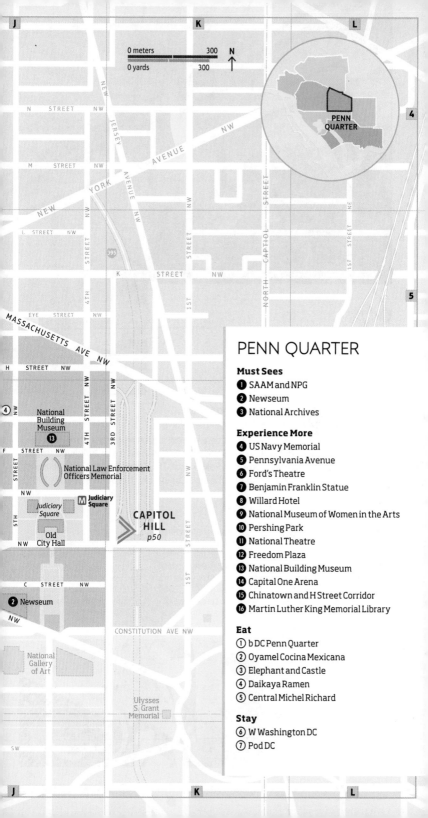

PENN QUARTER

Must Sees
1 SAAM and NPG
2 Newseum
3 National Archives

Experience More
4 US Navy Memorial
5 Pennsylvania Avenue
6 Ford's Theatre
7 Benjamin Franklin Statue
8 Willard Hotel
9 National Museum of Women in the Arts
10 Pershing Park
11 National Theatre
12 Freedom Plaza
13 National Building Museum
14 Capital One Arena
15 Chinatown and H Street Corridor
16 Martin Luther King Memorial Library

Eat
1 b DC Penn Quarter
2 Oyamel Cocina Mexicana
3 Elephant and Castle
4 Daikaya Ramen
5 Central Michel Richard

Stay
6 W Washington DC
7 Pod DC

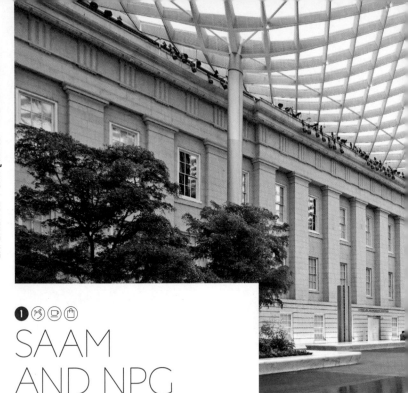

①ⓂⒹ🖐

SAAM AND NPG

📍H6 🏛8th & F Sts, NW Ⓜ Gallery Place-Chinatown
🕐11:30am-7pm daily 🆆americanart.si.edu, npg.si.edu

Two exceptional museums, the Smithsonian American Art Museum (SAAM) and the National Portrait Gallery (NPG), share one of the city's most iconic buildings, linked by a courtyard with a striking Norman Foster roof. The Greek Revival-style National Historic Landmark, once the Patent Office, was bought by the Smithsonian in 1958.

EXPLORING THE SAAM

The museum houses one of the world's largest collections of American art, illuminating the country's artistic and cultural history from the Colonial era to today. It is a matchless record of the American experience, capturing the identity, spirit, and dreams of people over the centuries. The SAAM holds significant aspects of visual culture, including African-American and Latino art. It also has important collections of contemporary art, American Impressionist paintings, and masterpieces from the Gilded Age, as well as the country's largest trove of New Deal art. Over 7,000 artists are represented in the collections. Among the highlights are 19th-century works by Winslow Homer; Impressionist art by Mary Cassatt; Modernist works by Georgia O'Keeffe; folk art by James Hampton; and contemporary works by Roy Lichtenstein and Christo.

→

The Thundershower (c 1917-18) by H. Lyman Saÿen, a mix of European Modernism and Native American patterns

←

The Kogod Courtyard linking the twin museums, a spectacular modern counterpoint to NPG's Great Hall *(inset)*

EXPLORING THE NPG

The NPG is America's family album, magnificently combining history, biography, and art in its collections. By highlighting "men and women who have made significant contributions to the history, development, and culture of the people of the United States," the gallery keeps generations of remarkable Americans in the company of their fellow citizens. There are presidents and people of God, visionaries and villains, artists and activists – all individuals who have shaped America's national identity. The portraits are fascinating not only because they reveal their subjects but also because they illustrate the times in which they were produced. There are more than 23,000 images in the permanent collection, which includes a variety of media, from paintings, photographs, and sculptures to digital works and time-based media.

INSIDER TIP
Lansdowne Portrait (1796)
Observe this life-size portrait carefully – Gilbert Stuart painted George Washington from life for this work, and later wrote that the president's constrained expression was because of his new false teeth.

→

Amy Sherald's 2018 portrait *First Lady Michelle Obama*, with a simple blue background evocative of American folk art

2 🔨 Ⓜ 🍴 🖥 🏛

NEWSEUM

📍J7 🏠 555 Pennsylvania Ave, NW Ⓜ Archives-Navy Memorial-Penn Quarter 🕐 9am-5pm Mon-Sat, 10am-5pm Sun 🚫 Jan 1, Thanksgiving, Dec 25 🌐 newseum.org

This award-winning news and media museum is dedicated to the positive role that journalism plays in defending democracy and freedom worldwide. Housed in a beautiful building with a balcony that affords splendid views of the city, the Newseum features seven levels, 14 galleries, and 15 theaters that explore how and why news is made. On the front of the building, the First Amendment, which guarantees freedom of speech, is engraved six stories tall.

The museum's collections span five centuries of news history, including cutting-edge technology and hands-on exhibits. One of the most popular galleries features decades of Pulitzer Prize-winning photographs, including the iconic 1945 image of the US flag at Iwo Jima and the 1969 photograph of the execution of a Viet Cong prisoner in Saigon, Vietnam. Other galleries deal with the history of the Berlin Wall and the events of 9/11, illustrating the varying goals of reportage on momentous or catastrophic events. A favorite is the interactive newsroom, where visitors can read the news off a teleprompter in front of a live TV camera. In January 2019, the museum was sold to the John Hopkins University, but will remain open to the public until the end of 2019.

Did You Know?

In addition to being a lawyer, Congressman, and US president, Lincoln was also a newspaper publisher.

The First Amendment on the facade listing the five freedoms: religion, speech, press, assembly, and petition →

1 The "Today's Front Pages" gallery displays about 80 of the more than 800 front pages that the Newseum receives every day.

2 The moving "Journalists Memorial" exhibit honors the sacrifices made by journalists around the world in their pursuit of the truth.

3 One of the most powerful exhibits here, these Berlin Wall panels represent the profound change a free press can bring about.

GREAT VIEW
From the Newseum

The Greenspun Terrace on Level 6 offers one of Washington's best views of Pennsylvania Avenue and the grand US Capitol building.

The Rotunda of Rights, with ↑ argon-filled cases holding the three Charters of Freedom

3

NATIONAL ARCHIVES

📍 H7 🏛 Constitution Ave between 7th & 9th Sts, NW Ⓜ Archives-Navy Memorial-Penn Quarter 🕐 10am-5:30pm daily 🚫 Thanksgiving, Dec 25 🌐 archives.gov

In the 1930s, Congress recognized the need to preserve the country's paper records before they deteriorated or were lost or destroyed. The result was the National Archives, opened in 1934, which house the US's most important historical and legal documents. These include the Constitution, the Declaration of Independence, and the Bill of Rights, as well as a 1297 copy of Magna Carta.

 INSIDER TIP
Beat the Queues

If you plan to visit the archives during high season (April-July), beat the queues by reserving timed-entry tickets ($1.50 each online). Allow 30 minutes for the Charters of Freedom, but another one or two hours for the rest of the exhibits, especially "Public Vaults."

Also here are millions of documents, photographs, films, and sound recordings going back over two centuries. A permanent exhibition, "Public Vaults," contains interactive displays and about 1,100 documents and artifacts, ranging from George Washington's letters and Abraham Lincoln's wartime telegrams to a recording of a speech by Theodore Roosevelt. The exhibit has five individual themes, including "We the People," with documents on family and citizenship, and "To Form a More Perfect Union," which displays records of Liberty and Law.

→

One of two 1936 murals by Barry Faulkner with fictional representations of the Declaration of Independence and US Constitution

EXPERIENCE MORE

❹ US Navy Memorial

⬛ H7 **Ⓜ Market Sq,
Pennsylvania Ave
between 7th & 9th
Sts, NW** **Ⓜ Archives-Navy
Memorial-Penn Quarter**

The memorial centers on
the statue of a single sailor
standing on a vast map of the
world. Sculpted in bronze by
Stanley Bleifeld in 1990, it is a
poignant tribute to the men
and women who have served
in the US Navy. Behind the
memorial, the **Naval Heritage
Center** has historical exhibits
and portraits of famous naval
personnel. A free film, *At Sea*,
is shown at 2pm.

Naval Heritage Center

Ⓒ **⬛ 701 Pennsylvania Ave,
NW** **Ⓒ 9:30am–5pm daily**
⬛ Jan 1, Thanksgiving, Dec 25
ⓦ navymemorial.org

❺ Pennsylvania Avenue

⬛ H7 **Ⓜ Pennsylvania
Ave** **Ⓜ Federal Triangle,
Archives-Navy Memorial-
Penn Quarter**

When the original architect of
Washington, Pierre L'Enfant,
drew up his plans in 1789 for
the capital of the new United
States, he imagined a grand
boulevard running through
the center of the city, from the
presidential palace to the
legislative building. For the
first 200 years of its history,
however, Pennsylvania
Avenue fell sadly short of his
dreams. In the early 19th century it was simply a muddy
footpath through the woods.
Paved in 1833, it became part
of a neighborhood of board-
ing houses, shops, and hotels.
During the Civil War, the street
deteriorated into an area of
saloons and gambling dens.

When President Kennedy's
inaugural parade proceeded
down the avenue in 1961, he
said, "It's a disgrace – fix it."
Congress was spurred to set
up a plan to revitalize the
area. Today, the avenue is a
clean, tree-lined street with
parks, memorials, theaters,
shops, hotels, museums, and
government buildings – a
suitably grand setting for all
inaugural parades.

↑ The US Capitol at the end
of Pennsylvania Avenue

250,000

filing cabinets can be
filled with the documents
housed in the National
Archives.

THE CONSTITUTION

Delegates from the
13 original American
states met in 1787 in
Philadelphia. Months
of debate followed
as they drafted the
framework for a new
country. Cooperation
and compromise finally
led to the creation of
the Constitution, which
outlines the powers of
the central government
and the makeup of
Congress. The majority
of states ratified the
document, giving up
some of their power in
"order to form a more
perfect union."

PRESIDENTIAL INAUGURAL PARADES

The tradition of inaugural parades to mark a new
president's coming-to-office started in 1809, when the
military accompanied President James Madison from his
Virginia home to Washington, DC. The first parade to
include floats was held in 1841 for President William
Henry Harrison. In 1985, freezing weather forced Ronald
Reagan's inaugural ceremony indoors to the Capitol
Rotunda. A record crowd of approximately 1.8 million
attended the 2009 parade for Barack Obama. The Army
Band traditionally leads the parade down Pennsylvania
Avenue from the US Capitol to the White House.

6

Ford's Theatre

◉ H6 ⬒ 511 10th St between E & F Sts, NW Ⓜ Gallery Place-Chinatown, Metro Center �◷ 9am–4:30pm daily with timed pass (except matinee or rehearsal days – call ahead) ⓦ fords.org

John T. Ford, a theatrical producer, built this small jewel of a theater in 1863. Washington was a Civil War boomtown, and the theater enjoyed great popularity. Its fate was sealed, however, on April 14, 1865, when President Abraham Lincoln was shot here by John Wilkes Booth while watching a performance. After the tragedy, people stopped patronizing the theater, and Ford was forced to sell the building. It was left to spiral into decay for nearly a century until the government decided to restore it to its original splendor. Today, the theater stages small productions and offers tours of the building, which looks much as it did in 1865. Across the street, visitors can tour **Petersen House**, where Lincoln died the next morning.

Petersen House
⍟ 9:30am–5:30pm daily with free timed ticket

Did You Know?

Despite only two years of formal education, Benjamin Franklin was a brilliant polymath and inventor.

7

Benjamin Franklin Statue

◉ H6 ⬒ Pennsylvania Ave & 10th St, NW Ⓜ Federal Triangle

Standing in front of the Old Post Office, this statue was unveiled by Franklin's great-granddaughter in 1889. The words "Printer, Philosopher, Patriot, Philanthropist" are inscribed on the four sides of the statue's pedestal. Postmaster General, writer, and scientist, Franklin was also a member of the committee that drafted the 1776 Declaration of Independence. As a diplomat to the court of Louis XVI of France, he went to Versailles in 1777 to gain support for the American cause of independence from Britain. Franklin returned to France in 1783 to negotiate the Treaty of Paris that ended the American Revolution.

8

Willard Hotel

◉ G6 ⬒ 1401 Pennsylvania Ave, NW Ⓜ Metro Center ⓦ washington.intercontinental.com

There has been a hotel on this site since 1816. Originally called Tennison's, the hotel occupied six adjacent two-story buildings. Refurbished in 1847, it was managed by Henry Willard, who gave his name to the hotel in 1850. Many famous people stayed here during the Civil War (1861–65), including Julia Ward Howe, who wrote the Civil War standard "The Battle Hymn of the Republic," and the writer Nathaniel Hawthorne. The word "lobbyist" is sometimes claimed to have been coined because it was known by those seeking favors that President Ulysses S. Grant went to the hotel's lobby to smoke his after-dinner cigar.

The present 330-room building was completed in 1904. It was the most popular place to stay in the city until the end of World War II, when the neighborhood fell into decline. For 20 years it was boarded up and faced demolition. A coalition worked to restore the Beaux Arts building, and it finally reopened in renewed splendor in 1986.

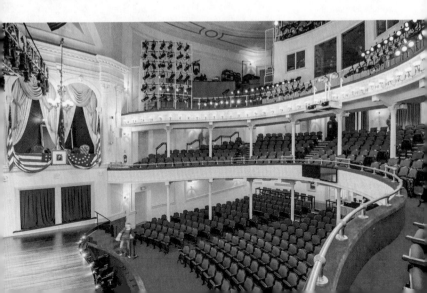

National Museum of Women in the Arts

📍H5 🏛1250 New York Ave, NW Ⓜ Metro Center 🕐10am-5pm Mon-Sat, noon-5pm Sun 🚫Jan 1, Thanksgiving, Dec 25 🌐nmwa.org

This museum of women's art houses works from the Renaissance to the present day. The superb collection was started in the 1960s by Wilhelmina Holladay and her husband, who picked up paintings, sculpture, and photography from all over the world. The museum operated out of their private residence for several years, until it acquired a more permanent home in this Renaissance Revival landmark building, formerly a Masonic Temple.

The collection's highlights include masterpieces by female American artists. Among the outstanding 19th-century works are *The Bath* (1891) by Mary Cassatt and *The Cage* (1885) by French artist Berthe Morisot. Among the works by 20th-century artists are Elizabeth Catlett's *Singing their Songs* (1992) and *Self-Portrait Between the Curtains, Dedication to Trotsky* (1937) by Mexican artist Frida Kahlo.

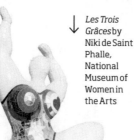

↓ *Les Trois Grâces* by Niki de Saint Phalle, National Museum of Women in the Arts

🔟

Pershing Park

📍G6 🏛Pennsylvania Ave & 15th St, NW Ⓜ Metro Center 🕐24 hrs daily 🌐nps.gov

While this park's official purpose is to honor World War I "General of the Armies," John J. Pershing, residents

Interior of Ford's Theatre, with the Presidential Box on the left

have discovered that the park is a cool, green oasis in the heart of DC. Here, a pond fed by a waterfall and surrounded by flowering shade trees is fronted by a plaza with comfortable benches. In the winter the pond becomes a popular ice-skating rink. Built in the 1970s as part of the renovation of Pennsylvania Avenue, the park is now managed by the National Park system, and includes a statue of General Pershing.

###

National Theatre

📍G6 🏛1321 Pennsylvania Ave, NW Ⓜ Metro Center, Federal Triangle 🌐thenationaldc.org

The National Theatre is the sixth theater to occupy this site and the oldest cultural institution in the city. The current building dates from 1922 and hosts Broadway-bound productions and touring groups. Known as an "actor's theater" because of its fine acoustics, the National is said to be haunted by the ghost of 19th-century actor John McCullough, killed by a fellow actor and buried under the stage. There are free performances for children every Saturday at 9:30am and 11am.

EAT

b DC Penn Quarter

A leather-and-brass eatery whose tagline "burgers, beer, and bourbon" says it all.

📍H7 🏛801 Pennsylvania Ave, NW 🌐burgersbeer bourbon.com

$⑤⑤⑤

Oyamel Cocina Mexicana

Trendy, upscale, and creative Mexican small plates, with an extensive drinks menu.

📍J6 🏛401 7th St, NW 🌐oyamel.com

$⑤⑤⑤

Elephant and Castle

Family-oriented English pub with famed fish and chips and lots of beers.

📍H6 🏛1201 Pennsylvania Ave, NW 🌐elephantcastle.com

$⑤⑤⑤

Daikaya Ramen

Busy little shop known for its authentic Japanese ramen noodles.

📍J6 🏛705 6th St, NW 🌐daikaya.com

$⑤⑤⑤

Central Michel Richard

Modern American and French bistro with delightful entrees plus extensive drinks menu.

📍H6 🏛1001 Pennsylvania Ave, NW 🌐centralmichel richard.com

$⑤⑤⑤

12 Freedom Plaza

📍 G6 🏛 Pennsylvania Ave between 13th & 14th Sts, NW Ⓜ Federal Triangle, Metro Center

Freedom Plaza was conceived as part of the Pennsylvania Avenue redevelopment plan in the mid-1970s. Completed in 1980, it shows L'Enfant's original plan for Washington in black and white stone inlaid in the ground. Around the edge are engraved quotations about the city from President Wilson and Walt Whitman, among others. To the north of the plaza, where Pennsylvania Avenue leads into E Street, are the Warner Theatre and the National Theatre. South of the plaza is the Beaux Arts District Building (housing government employees). The plaza is also a popular site for festivals and political protests.

STAY

W Washington DC
This elegant, upscale boutique hotel is set near the White House. Great views from the rooftop lounge.

📍 G6 🏛 515 15th St, NW 🌐 wwashingtondc.com

$$$

Pod DC
Small rooms, good beds, and essential amenities keep rates affordable. There's a diner, rooftop lounge, and free access to nearby fitness and shared-work spaces.

📍 J5 🏛 627 H St, NW 🌐 thepodhotel.com/pod-dc

$$$

13 National Building Museum

📍 J6 🏛 401 F St at 4th St, NW Ⓜ Judiciary Square, Gallery Place-Chinatown ⏰ 10am-5pm Mon-Sat, 11am-5pm Sun 🚫 Jan 1, Thanksgiving, Dec 25 🌐 nbm.org

It is fitting that the National Building Museum, dedicated to the building trade, should be housed in the architecturally audacious former Pension Bureau building. It is based on Michelangelo's Palazzo Farnese, but is twice as big and in red brick as opposed to the stone masonry of the Rome original.

Completed in 1887, the vast concourse, measuring 316 ft by 116 ft (96 m by 35 m), is lined with balconies and has huge columns of plastered brick, faux-painted to give the appearance of marble. The Great Hall has been the venue for many presidential balls.

The building fell on hard times in the 1920s but was eventually restored, reopening in 1985 in renewed splendor as the National Building Museum. The museum features temporary exhibits on buildings and architecture, and a permanent exhibition on the architectural history of Washington, DC. For children under six, the "Building Zone" offers some hands-on fun, including giant LEGO blocks, bulldozers, and a playhouse.

14 Capital One Arena

📍 J6 🏛 601 F St, NW Ⓜ Gallery Place-Chinatown ⏰ 10am-5:30pm daily, later on event days (team store) 🌐 capitalonearena.com

Opened in 1997, the Capital One Arena is a sports and entertainment complex that houses many shops and restaurants. Its 20,000-seat stadium is the home of the city's basketball teams, the Wizards (men's team), the Mystics (women's), and the Georgetown Hoyas, as well as the ice hockey team, the Capitals. The presence of the complex has revived the surrounding area beyond recognition. It also hosts rock concerts as well as sports events and exhibitions.

---

15 Chinatown and H Street Corridor

📍 J5 🏛 Between 5th to 8th Sts & H to I St, NW Ⓜ Gallery Place-Chinatown

The small area in Washington known as Chinatown covers just six square blocks. Formed around 1930, it has never been very large and today houses

→

A colorful dragon parade in Washington's Chinatown district

The huge columns of the National Building Museum concourse

about 500 Chinese residents. The area was reinvigorated with the arrival of the adjacent Capital One Arena in 1997.

The Friendship Archway, a dramatic gateway that spans H Street at the junction with 7th Street, marks the center of Chinatown. Built in 1986 as a gift from Beijing, it is the largest single-span Chinese arch in the world. During the Chinese New Year celebrations, the area comes alive with a colorful parade, dragon dances, and live musical performances (p42).

Chinatown is at the western end of a 1.5-mile (2.5-km) stretch of H Street that has undergone a remarkable revitalization. Multicultural neighborhoods have become incubators of a vibrant arts, music, and culinary scene, and the street is alive with shops, galleries, and restaurants. The anchor for this neighborhood is the historic Atlas Center for the Performing Arts, which stages award-winning shows.

(p42)

DR. MARTIN LUTHER KING, JR.

A charismatic speaker, advocate of Gandhi's theories of non-violence, and Nobel Peace Prize winner, Dr. King (1929–68) was a black Baptist minister and civil rights leader. At the March on Washington in 1963, 200,000 people gathered at the Lincoln Memorial to hear King's "I Have a Dream" speech. Congress passed significant civil rights legislation the next year.

Martin Luther King Memorial Library

H6 **901 G St at 9th St, NW** **Gallery Place-Chinatown, Metro Center** **Closed for restoration until 2020** **dclibrary.org/mlk**

The Martin Luther King Memorial Library is the city's only example of the Modernist architecture of Ludwig Mies van der Rohe. A key figure in 20th-century design, van der Rohe finalized the library plans shortly before his death in 1969. It was named in honor of Dr. King when it opened in 1972, replacing the Carnegie Library as the city's central public library. Architecturally, the building is an austere, simple box with a recessed entrance lobby. Inside, there is a mural by artist Don Miller depicting Dr. King's life. The library sponsors numerous concerts and readings, as well as children's events.

A SHORT WALK
PENN QUARTER

Distance 1.2 miles (2 km) **Nearest Metro** Federal Triangle
Time 25 minutes

The main route for presidential inaugural parades, Pennsylvania Avenue is a grand boulevard worthy of L'Enfant's original vision. This spacious thoroughfare links the White House to the US Capitol and is home to some of the city's main sights. The Mellon Fountain and Newseum are at the intersection with 6th Street, NW. Opposite the US Navy Memorial is the US National Archives, housing original copies of the Constitution and the Declaration of Independence. Benjamin Franklin's statue stands in front of the Old Post Office, and the National Museum of Women in The Arts is on the corner of 12th Street, NW.

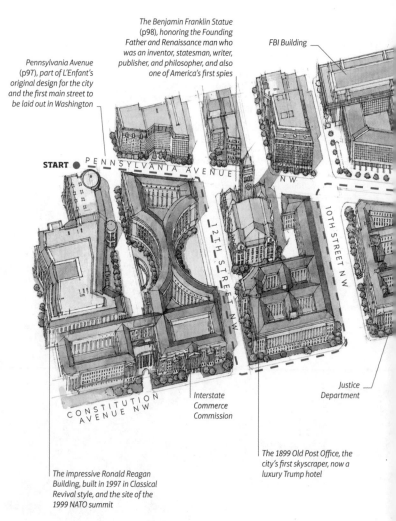

The Benjamin Franklin Statue (p98), honoring the Founding Father and Renaissance man who was an inventor, statesman, writer, publisher, and philosopher, and also one of America's first spies

FBI Building

Pennsylvania Avenue (p97), part of L'Enfant's original design for the city and the first main street to be laid out in Washington

START

PENNSYLVANIA AVENUE NW

12TH STREET NW

10TH STREET NW

Justice Department

CONSTITUTION AVENUE NW

Interstate Commerce Commission

The 1899 Old Post Office, the city's first skyscraper, now a luxury Trump hotel

The impressive Ronald Reagan Building, built in 1997 in Classical Revival style, and the site of the 1999 NATO summit

↑ The imposing United States Capitol seen from Pennsylvania Avenue

Locator Map
For more detail see p90

0 meters 50 N
0 yards 50

The Newseum (p94), presenting the story of news and demonstrating how the US First Amendment freedoms impact daily life

6TH STREET NW

7TH STREET NW

PENNSYLVANIA AVENUE NW

9TH STREET NW

FINISH

CONSTITUTION AVENUE NW

Federal Trade Commission

The Mellon Fountain, located across Constitution Avenue, NW from the National Gallery of Art's West Building and named after Andrew Mellon, an industrialist and art collector who founded the gallery in the 1930s

The National Archives (p96), home to the nation's most precious documents, known as the Charters of Freedom

The US Navy Memorial (p97), paved with a huge map of the world and surrounded by low granite walls, statuary, and fountains

→ The Neo-Classical building of the National Archives, designed by John Russell Pope in the early 1930s

WHITE HOUSE AND FOGGY BOTTOM

In 1800 the American government moved from Philadelphia to Washington. The city was a near wilderness, with only a scattering of simple buildings and chickens, cows, and pigs wandering the mud streets. Nonetheless, John Adams and his wife Abigail took up residence in the new President's House, designed by James Hoban. Although burned down by the British during the War of 1812, most of today's building remains as it was planned and is still the heart of the area. Visitors without pre-arranged tour tickets can still stroll around the building, taking in the views of the lovely North and South porticoes. West of the White House is the Foggy Bottom area. Built on swampland near the confluence of the Potomac and Rock Creek, it is said to have gained its name from the industries of the 19th century and an atmospheric quirk that funneled fog in. The area became home to George Washington University in the early 20th century, and also boasts the cutting-edge Kennedy Center, with its year-round calendar of celebrated performances.

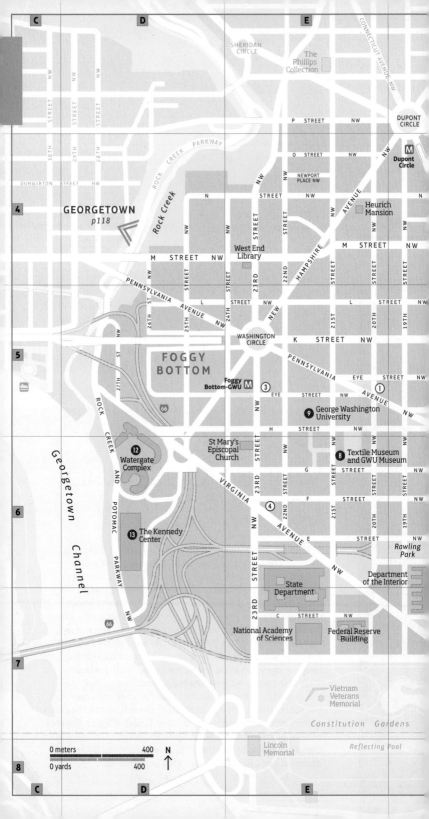

WHITE HOUSE AND FOGGY BOTTOM

Must See
1 White House

Experience More
2 Lafayette Square
3 Treasury Building
4 Hay-Adams Hotel
5 St. John's Church
6 Renwick Gallery
7 Octagon House Museum
8 Textile Museum and GWU Museum
9 George Washington University
10 Organization of American States
11 National Geographic Museum
12 Watergate Complex
13 The Kennedy Center

Eat
1 El Chalan
2 GCDC Grilled Cheese Bar
3 CIRCA

Stay
4 Hotel Hive
5 Mayflower Hotel

NORTHWEST
p146

MASSACHUSETTS AVENUE NW

RHODE ISLAND AVE NW

SCOTT CIRCLE

STREET NW

CONNECTICUT AVENUE NW

DESALES STREET NW

M STREET NW

National Geographic Museum

L STREET NW

Farragut North M

K STREET NW

Farragut West M

FARRAGUT SQUARE

EYE STREET

McPHERSON SQUARE

McPherson Square M

Hay-Adams Hotel

St. John's Church

H STREET NW

Renwick Gallery

Lafayette Square

Eisenhower Old Executive Office Building

PENNSYLVANIA AVENUE NW

Octagon House Museum

White House

Treasury Building

PENN QUARTER
p88

Corcoran Gallery of Art

Daughters of the American Revolution

The Ellipse

Organization of American States

ELLIPSE ROAD NW

CONSTITUTION AVENUE NW

THE MALL
p62

THE MALL

World War II Memorial

Washington Monument

Constitution Gardens

Metro Center M

National Theatre

FREEDOM PLAZA

White House Visitor Center

Ronald Reagan Building

Ford's Theatre

FBI Building

PENNSYLVANIA AVENUE NW

Federal Triangle M

WHITE HOUSE AND FOGGY BOTTOM

① Ⓜ 🛍

WHITE HOUSE

📍G6 🏛White House: 1600 Pennsylvania Ave, NW; visitor center: 1450 Pennsylvania Ave, NW Ⓜ Federal Triangle ⏰White House: Tue–Sat; visitor center: 7:30am–4pm daily 🚫White House: Federal holidays, official functions; visitor center: Jan 1, Thanksgiving, Dec 25 🌐nps.gov/whho

With every US president except George Washington having called the White House home, this Neo-Classical mansion has been the seat of executive power for over 200 years.

One of the most famous residential landmarks in the world, the White House was built to reflect the power of the presidency. Although George Washington commissioned the mansion, President John Adams was its first occupant, in 1800. In 1902, President Theodore Roosevelt ordered the West Wing to be built, and in 1942 the East Wing was added by President Franklin D. Roosevelt, completing the building as it is today.

TOP 5 DECORATIVE FEATURES

China Room Collection
A collection of family and state china from nearly every president.

Monroe Plateau
A 14.5-ft- (4.5-m-) long French gilt table service.

Grand Staircase
Used for ceremonial entrances and presidential portraits.

North Entrance Carvings
Finely made door surround carved with flowing garlands of roses and acorns.

Vermeil Room
A display of "vermeil", gilded objects by 19th-century silversmiths, and several portraits of First Ladies.

→

The White House facade, and the Diplomatic Reception room *(inset)*, with its famous Zuber "Views of North America" block printed wallpaper

EXPERIENCE White House and Foggy Bottom

Timeline

1792
△ George Washington supervises the construction of the mansion; in 1814, it is burned down by the British during the War of 1812.

1901
△ The structure is renamed the White House by Theodore Roosevelt; his successor, William Taft *(above)*, creates the first Oval Office in 1909.

1948
△ Harry Truman begins a major reconstruction of the building in which absolutely everything except the outer walls is dismantled.

2013
△ Barack Obama installs solar panels on the roof, the first time solar power is used for a president's living quarters.

Did You Know?

570 gallons (2,100 liters) of paint are needed to cover the exterior of the White House.

Exploring the White House

The 132 rooms in the White House, beautifully decorated in period styles and filled with valuable antique furniture, china, and silverware, preserve the cultural and political touchstones of America's past and present. Hanging on their walls are some of America's most treasured paintings, including portraits of past presidents and First Ladies. To tour the White House, you must start the process well before your visit. US citizens must request tickets from their Member of Congress. The request can be made up to three months in advance, but at the very minimum tickets must be requested 21 days in advance. Foreign citizens must make a request for tickets at their embassy in DC. Those without tour tickets can experience a virtual tour at the White House Visitor Center.

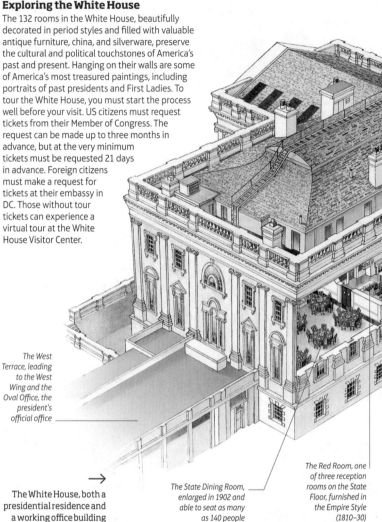

The West Terrace, leading to the West Wing and the Oval Office, the president's official office

→

The White House, both a presidential residence and a working office building

The State Dining Room, enlarged in 1902 and able to seat as many as 140 people

The Red Room, one of three reception rooms on the State Floor, furnished in the Empire Style (1810–30)

FLIPPING THE WHITE HOUSE

On Inauguration Day, the White House must be changed over for the incoming president in just five hours. At 10:30am the outgoing family leaves for the inauguration, and the carefully choreographed chaos begins. The outgoing family's moving trucks park on South Portico's west side, and the incoming family's on the east. The rooms are scrubbed, rugs and curtains cleaned, repairs made, all personal belongings placed, and the Oval Office painted. At 3:30pm the new First Family arrives, and the Chief Usher says, "Welcome to your new home, Mr. President."

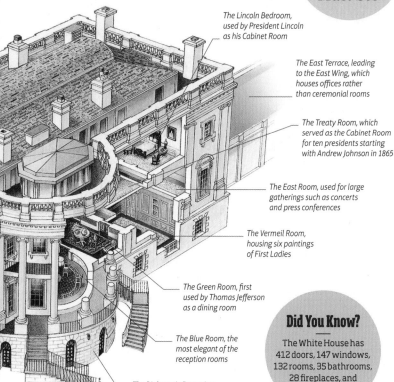

The Lincoln Bedroom, used by President Lincoln as his Cabinet Room

The East Terrace, leading to the East Wing, which houses offices rather than ceremonial rooms

The Treaty Room, which served as the Cabinet Room for ten presidents starting with Andrew Johnson in 1865

The East Room, used for large gatherings such as concerts and press conferences

The Vermeil Room, housing six paintings of First Ladies

The Green Room, first used by Thomas Jefferson as a dining room

The Blue Room, the most elegant of the reception rooms

The Diplomatic Reception room, furnished in Federal style (1790–1820)

Did You Know?

The White House has 412 doors, 147 windows, 132 rooms, 35 bathrooms, 28 fireplaces, and 8 staircases.

1 Every president personalizes the Oval Office – Obama added a bust of Martin Luther King, Jr., while Trump added a bust of Winston Churchill and military flags.

2 The State Dining Room mantel has a portrait of President Lincoln.

3 The Red Room, decorated by Jacqueline Kennedy, is used as a sitting room and for small parties.

EXPERIENCE MORE

Lafayette Square

📍 G6 Ⓜ Farragut West, McPherson Square
🌐 nps.gov

Behind the White House is Lafayette Square, named for the Marquis de Lafayette (1757–1834), a hero of the Revolutionary War. Due to its proximity to the White House, this park is often the scene of peaceful demonstrations. It is also home to 19th-century mansions and the historic St. John's, "Church of the Presidents." In the center of the square is a huge statue of President Andrew Jackson (1767–1845), and at its four corners stand statues of men who took part in America's struggle for liberty. The southeast corner honors Lafayette. In the southwest is Jean-Baptiste Donatien de Vimeur, Comte de Rochambeau (1725–1807). Baron von Steuben (1730–94), Washington's aide at Valley Forge, is honored in the northwest end. Polish general Thaddeus Kosciuszko (1746–1817), who fought in the Revolutionary War, stands in the northeast.

↑ A bronze seal from 1789 on display at the Treasury Building

Treasury Building

📍 G6 🏛 Pennsylvania Ave & 15th St, NW
Ⓜ McPherson Square
🌐 treasury.gov

This grand four-story Greek Revival edifice was designed by architect Robert Mills, who also designed the Washington Monument (p83). A statue of Alexander Hamilton, the first Secretary of the Treasury, stands at the southern entrance to the building. The official guided tour takes in the restored historic rooms, including the 1864 burglar-proof vault and the marble Cash Room. Between 1863 and 1880, US currency was printed in the basement. Today, the building is home to the Department of the Treasury, which manages the government's finances and protects US financial systems.

Hay-Adams Hotel

📍 F5 🏛 1 Lafayette Sq, NW
Ⓜ Farragut North, Farragut West
🌐 hayadams.com

Situated close to the White House, this historic hotel is a city landmark built in Italian Renaissance style and with an interior adorned with beautiful European and Oriental antiques. Originally two adjacent houses, built by Henry Hobson Richardson in 1885 for statesman John Hay and diplomat Henry Adams, it has been a popular hotel since its 1927 conversion and remains one of Washington's top establishments, well sited for all the major sights. Drop in for afternoon tea at the Lafayette Restaurant.

EAT

El Chalan

Authentic Peruvian cuisine served in a cozy, white-tablecloth dining room with photos of Peru on the walls.

 E5 📍 1924 I St, NW 🕐 Sun & L Sat 🌐 elchalandc.com

$$$

GCDC Grilled Cheese Bar

Near the White House, this cheese-centric eatery serves grilled cheese sandwiches, including the French onion and buffalo blue.

📍 F6 📍 1730 Pennsylvania Ave, NW 🕐 Sun & from 6pm Sat 🌐 grilledcheesedc.com

$$$

CIRCA

Trendy bistro with creative New American fare and drinks, and indoor and patio dining.

📍 E5 📍 2221 I St, NW 🌐 circabistros.com

$$$

St. John's Church

📍 G5 📍 16th & H Sts, NW at Lafayette Sq Ⓜ McPherson Square 🕐 1–3pm daily 🌐 stjohns-dc.org

This graceful, historic church has hosted every sitting US president since James Madison. Built in 1816, it has a simple yet elegant interior

Statue of Andrew Jackson in the center of Lafayette Square

An elegant interior in the Octagon House Museum, restored to its 1815 appearance

with 22 beautiful stained-glass memorial windows. A guided tour is offered after the 11am service on Sunday.

Renwick Gallery

📍 F6 📍 Pennsylvania Ave at 17th St, NW Ⓜ Farragut West 🕐 10am–5:30pm daily 🌐 americanart.si.edu

Part of the Smithsonian American Art Museum *(p92)*, this elegant redbrick building was designed and constructed by James Renwick Jr. in 1858. It originally housed the collection of banker William Wilson Corcoran and was later bought by the Smithsonian, refurbished, and reopened as the Renwick Gallery in 1972.

The gallery's mission is to conserve and display the Smithsonian's collection of 20th-century and contemporary American arts, crafts, and design. Highlights of the collection include superb examples of American craftsmanship, such as master woodworker Wendell Castle's *Ghost Clock*, a wooden piece that looks like a grandfather clock draped in delicate linen, and Larry Fuente's *Game Fish*, a large sculptural sailfish that is encrusted with toy and game pieces such as dice and ping-pong balls.

Octagon House Museum

📍 F6 📍 1799 New York Ave, NW Ⓜ Farragut West, Farragut North 🕐 1–4pm Thu–Sat 🕐 Jan 1, Thanksgiving, Dec 25 🌐 octagonmuseum.org

Actually hexagonal in shape, the Octagon is a three-story redbrick building designed in the late-Federal style by Dr. William Thornton (1759–1828), first architect of the US Capitol. It was completed in 1801 for Colonel John Tayloe III, a plantation owner and a friend of George Washington. After the White House was burned down in the War of 1812 against Britain, President James Madison and his wife Dolley lived here from 1814 to 1815.

Octagon House has been fully restored to its historically accurate 1815 appearance and now houses an architectural museum run by the American Institute of Architects. Visitors can take self-guided tours, and unlike most other fine home museums, here they are encouraged to touch and use furnishings, lie on the rope bed, or play a game of whist in the drawing room. The house is full of fine architectural features, including an impressive circular entrance hall.

Artifacts on display at the Textile Museum, including shoes (inset), garments, and fabric ↑

Textile Museum and GWU Museum

📍E6 🏛701 21st St, NW Ⓜ Foggy Bottom-GWU, Farragut North 🕐11am-5pm Mon, Fri, & Sat, 11am-7pm Wed & Thu, 1-5pm Sun 🚫University hols 🌐museum.gwu.edu

This unusual museum holds one of the world's finest collections of rugs, tapestries, and other textiles representing worldwide cultures and spanning over 5,000 years. Created in 1929 by George Hewitt Myers, the collection now has over 20,000 items. Among the highlights are 15th-century Mamluk carpets from Egypt, indigenous American weavings dating back to 900 BC, and Islamic textiles dating to the 9th century. There is also an extensive library featuring 20,000 books and publications focused on the current and historical theme of textiles.

The GWU Museum in the same building hosts the Albert H. Small Washingtoniana collection of artworks, publications, pamphlets, and other artifacts that relate the city's story from pre-Revolutionary times to the present.

George Washington University

📍E5 🏛2121 I (Eye) St, NW Ⓜ Foggy Bottom-GWU 🌐gwu.edu

Founded in 1821, George Washington University, known as "GW," is named after the first president of the United States. The largest university in DC, it has nine schools offering both undergraduate and graduate studies.

As a result of its location, GW has many famous alumni, including General Colin Powell (Secretary of State in George W. Bush's administration) and Jacqueline Bouvier (who married John Kennedy) as well as a number of children of past presidents. On-campus auditoriums host a series of plays, dances, lectures, and concerts.

Organization of American States

📍F7 🏛201 18th St, NW Ⓜ Farragut West 🕐10am-5pm Tue-Sun 🚫Federal hols

Dating back to the First International Conference

of the American States, held from October 1889 to April 1890 in Washington, the Organization of American States (OAS) is the oldest alliance of nations dedicated to reinforcing the continent's peace and security and maintaining democracy. The Charter of the OAS was signed in 1948 in Bogotá, Colombia, by the US and 20 Latin American republics. Today there are 35 members. The building houses the Columbus Memorial Library and the **Art Museum of the Americas**, which exhibits 20th-century Caribbean and Latin American art.

Art Museum of the Americas

🏛201 18th St, NW 🕐10am-5pm Tue-Sun 🚫Good Friday, Federal hols 🌐museum.oas.org

→

The distinctive curves of Washington's infamous Watergate Complex

National Geographic Museum

📍 F4 🏛 1145 17th St, NW
Ⓜ Farragut North, Farragut West 🕐 10am–6pm daily
🌐 nationalgeographic. org/dc

This small museum is located in the National Geographic Society's headquarters, designed by Edward Durrell Stone, the architect behind the Kennedy Center. A series of permanent and temporary exhibitions documents the richness of nature and the diversity of human culture all over the world.

Watergate Complex

📍 D6 🏛 Virginia Ave between Rock Creek Pkwy & New Hampshire Ave, NW
Ⓜ Foggy Bottom-GWU

Located next to the Kennedy Center, on the Potomac River, the impressive Watergate Complex was completed in 1971. Its four rounded buildings contain shops, offices, apartments, hotels, and diplomatic missions.

In 1972 the complex found itself at the center of international news when burglars, linked to President Nixon, broke into the Democratic National Committee offices, sparking off the Watergate scandal that led to the president's resignation.

The stunningly renovated Watergate Hotel reopened to rave reviews in 2016. The hotel has turned the infamous room 214 into a combination of luxury hotel room and museum. For a price varying between $600 and $1,000 a night, guests can occupy the actual room from which the 1972 break-in was supervised.

The Kennedy Center

📍 D6 🏛 New Hampshire Ave & Rock Creek Pkwy, NW
Ⓜ Foggy Bottom-GWU 🕐 10am–9pm daily
🌐 kennedy-center.org

In 1958, President Dwight D. Eisenhower signed an act to begin fundraising for a national cultural center that would attract the world's best orchestras, opera, and dance companies to the US capital. President John F. Kennedy was an ardent supporter of the arts, taking the lead in fundraising for it. He never saw the completion of the center, which was named in his honor.

Designed by Edward Durrell Stone, the center was opened on September 8, 1971 and houses several huge theaters: the Opera House, the Concert Hall, the Eisenhower Theater, and the Family Theater. On the roof are the Jazz Club, the Terrace Theater, and the Theater Lab. The Grand Foyer stretches 630 ft (192 m) and is home to the hugely popular Millennium Stage, which presents a wide range of free, family-friendly performances every evening at 6pm. In 2018, the center underwent its first renovation in over 50 years, adding more exciting venues to its riverfront area.

A SHORT WALK
AROUND THE
WHITE HOUSE

Distance 2 miles (3 km) **Nearest Metro** McPherson Square **Time** 35 minutes

The area surrounding the White House is filled with grand architecture and political history, and the vistas from the Ellipse lawn are breathtaking. The nearby Octagon House was built in 1801 for Colonel John Tayloe, and St. John's Church opened in 1816 when James Madison was president. The Renwick Gallery now occupies the first building in the nation that was built to be a museum, but before it was completed it was used by the Union Army during the Civil War. The building opened as the Corcoran Gallery of Art in 1874. Nearby is the Eisenhower Executive Office Building, which was the world's largest office building when it opened in 1888.

The Renwick Gallery, with an inscription above the entrance reading "Dedicated to Art"

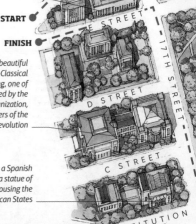

The Eisenhower Executive Office Building, completed in 1888 and now housing staff of the Executive branch

The Octagon Museum, at various times the home of fourth US president James Madison, a hospital, and a school

The Corcoran Gallery of Art, featuring select pieces from the original Corcoran Collection and the National Gallery of Art

START

FINISH

Did You Know?

The Ellipse was used for baseball games from the 1860s onwards and is still used for amateur sports.

The beautiful Neo-Classical DAR Building, one of three founded by the historical organization, the Daughters of the American Revolution

The 1910 OAS Building, a Spanish Colonial-style mansion, with a statue of Isabella of Spain outside, housing the Organization of American States

The luxurious Hay-Adams Hotel, the scene of political activity since it opened in the 1920s

St. John's Church, known as the "Church of Presidents" as every president since James Madison has attended services here

Locator Map
For more detail see p108

Leafy Lafayette Square, named after the Revolutionary War hero the Marquis de Lafayette, with a central statue of Andrew Jackson sculpted by Clark Mills

The White House, one of the most famous sights in Washington and the US president's official residence since the 1800s

STREET

MADISON PLACE

PENNSYLVANIA AVENUE

Treasury Building

A. HAMILTON PLACE

15TH STREET

E STREET

EXECUTIVE AVENUE

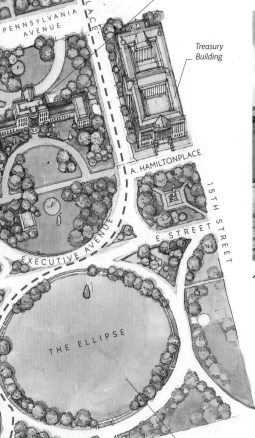

THE ELLIPSE

↑ The Treasury Building, built over 33 years and widely regarded as one of the most impressive Neo-Classical structures in the city

The Ellipse, site of the annual National Christmas Tree (p43) and the Zero Milestone from which all DC distances are measured

0 meters   100
0 yards   100

N

GEORGETOWN

Georgetown developed well before Washington, DC. Native Americans had a settlement here, and in 1703 a land grant was given to Ninian Beall, who named the area the Rock of Dumbarton. By the mid-18th century immigrants from Scotland had swelled the population, and in 1751 the town was renamed George Town. It grew rapidly into a wealthy tobacco and flour port and finally, in 1789, the city of Georgetown was formed. The harbor and the Chesapeake and Ohio Canal were built in 1828, and the streets were lined with townhouses. The birth of the railroad undercut Georgetown's economy, which by the mid-1800s was in decline. But by the 1950s the cobblestoned streets and charming houses were attracting wealthy young couples, and restaurants and shops sprang up on Wisconsin Avenue and M Street. Today Georgetown retains its sophisticated distinction from the rest of the city, and is a pleasant area in which to stroll for a few hours.

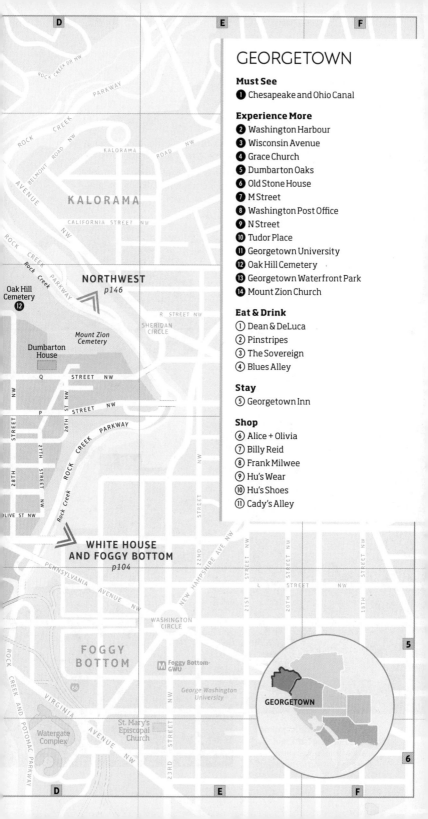

GEORGETOWN

Must See

❶ Chesapeake and Ohio Canal

Experience More

❷ Washington Harbour
❸ Wisconsin Avenue
❹ Grace Church
❺ Dumbarton Oaks
❻ Old Stone House
❼ M Street
❽ Washington Post Office
❾ N Street
❿ Tudor Place
⓫ Georgetown University
⓬ Oak Hill Cemetery
⓭ Georgetown Waterfront Park
⓮ Mount Zion Church

Eat & Drink

① Dean & DeLuca
② Pinstripes
③ The Sovereign
④ Blues Alley

Stay

⑤ Georgetown Inn

Shop

⑥ Alice + Olivia
⑦ Billy Reid
⑧ Frank Milwee
⑨ Hu's Wear
⑩ Hu's Shoes
⑪ Cady's Alley

1 🍴

CHESAPEAKE AND OHIO CANAL

📍 C5 🚪 From 29th & M Sts, NW in Georgetown to Cumberland, MD Ⓜ Foggy Bottom-GWU, then 15-min walk 🚌 31, 33 🕐 Sunrise–sunset daily 🌐 nps.gov/choh

The 184-mile (296-km) Chesapeake and Ohio Canal National Historical Park attracts over five million visitors who come to walk, jog, or bike along the towpath, canoe or kayak along the canal, or just enjoy the park's natural beauty.

Constructed between 1828 and 1850, the Chesapeake and Ohio Canal (C&O Canal) connected Georgetown to the rich farmlands of Cumberland, Maryland, and incorporated a revolutionary system of locks, aqueducts, and tunnels that allowed inland farmers to ship their produce quickly to eastern cities. With the arrival of the railroad in the late 19th century, the canal fell out of use, and became a national park in 1971. The most popular section is the 3-mile (5-km) stretch from M Street to Fletcher's Boat House, with picnic areas, great fishing, and boat rentals, and historic Abner Cloud House just across the towpath. Great Falls is also popular, with hiking and canal boat rides.

Did You Know?

A gongoozler is someone who likes to sit and idly watch the activity on a canal.

↑ The serene canal, with costumed guides offering 19th-century-style mule-drawn canal boat rides on some stretches *(inset)*

① The easiest way to enjoy the park is to walk, jog, or cycle along the canal towpath through Georgetown and west to Fletcher's Boat House.

② The Potomac creates a dramatic sight as it cascades through rocky Mather Gorge at Great Falls. Visitors come to hike the trails, take a canal boat ride, and learn about the history.

③ Canoeing and kayaking are popular on the C&O and are best between Georgetown and Violette's Lock – the first 22 miles (35 km) of the canal.

GEORGE'S CANAL

George Washington was the first to see the potential of linking the Potomac and the Ohio River Valley to transport goods. After his presidency, he set up the Patowmack Company, which built skirting canals around Great Falls. The project was completed after his death, and was superseded 26 years later by the C&O Canal.

↑ Patowmack Canal cargo toll cards

EXPERIENCE MORE

2

Washington Harbour

Q C5 **A** 3000-3020 K St, NW **M** Foggy Bottom-GWU, then 15-min walk **W** the washingtonharbour.com

Washington Harbour architect Arthur Cotton Moore created an unusually audacious development on the Potomac in 1981, with five large residential and commercial buildings that tower above the waterfront and surround a large open plaza ringed with shops and restaurants. The plaza also features a huge fountain that becomes a popular ice-skating rink in winter.

This is a great place to walk along the pleasant waterfront boardwalk, to dine inside or outside overlooking the water, or just sit and watch boats of all types make their way along the Potomac. A walkway follows the river and leads to the adjacent Georgetown Waterfront Park. The area's popularity and success eventually set the stage for much larger developments like District Wharf (p136) and National Harbor (p173) that have lately revitalized the city's waterfront areas.

Did You Know?

Wisconsin Avenue follows an ancient Native American trail, and first appeared on a map in 1712.

3

Wisconsin Avenue

Q C4 **A** Wisconsin Ave **M** Foggy Bottom-GWU

Wisconsin Avenue is one of two main business streets in Georgetown and is home to a wide variety of trendsetting shops and restaurants. It is also one of the few streets in Washington that predates L'Enfant's grid plan. It starts at the bank of the Potomac and runs north through Georgetown right to the city line, where it continues as Rockville Pike. On the junction of Wisconsin Avenue and M Street is the landmark gold dome of PNC Bank (formerly the Riggs National Bank). During the French and Indian Wars, George Washington marched his troops up the avenue on his way to Pittsburgh to engage the French forces.

4

Grace Church

Q C5 **A** 1041 Wisconsin Ave, NW **M** Foggy Bottom-GWU, Rosslyn, then 20-min walk **◷** 10am-4pm Mon-Fri, 8am-noon & 5-6:30pm Sun **W** gracedc.org

Built in 1866, Grace Church was designed to serve the boatmen who worked on the Chesapeake and Ohio Canal (p122) and the sailors of the port of Georgetown. Set on a tree-filled plot south of the canal and M Street, the Gothic Revival church, with its quaint exterior, is an oasis of calm in Georgetown. As the building has undergone few alterations over the years, it has a certain timeless quality. The church's multiethnic congregation makes great efforts to reach out to the larger DC community and works with soup kitchens and shelters for the homeless. In addition, the church sponsors the "Thank God It's Friday" lunchtime discussion group, and holds a poetry coffee house on the

Washington Harbour ↓

↑ Lush fig plants among the abundant greenery in the Orangery at Dumbarton Oaks

third Tuesday of the month. Classical concerts, including chamber pieces, organ, and piano works, are held regularly. There is also a popular annual festival devoted to German composer J. S. Bach.

Dumbarton Oaks

📍 C2 🏠 1703 32nd St, NW
Ⓜ Foggy Bottom-GWU, Dupont Circle, then bus
🕐 House: 11:30am–5pm Tue–Sun; gardens: 2–6pm Tue–Sun (to 5pm Nov–Feb)
🚫 Federal hols 🌐 doaks.org

Originally built in 1801 by Senator William Dorsey of Maryland, this fine Federal-style home was overgrown and neglected when it was purchased by pharmaceutical heirs Robert and Mildred Woods Bliss in 1920. The Blisses lovingly restored and modernized the house to meet 20th-century family needs. They also wanted their home to be surrounded by superb gardens, so they engaged their friend, Beatrix Jones Farrand, one of the few female landscape architects at the time, to lay out the grounds. Farrand's design began with lush formal gardens close to the house, and

slowly became less structured further away, eventually blending in with the surrounding woodlands.

The Blisses were also avid collectors of Byzantine art, and in 1940, when they moved to California, they donated their whole estate to Harvard University. It was then converted into a library, research institution, and museum, where many of the pieces on display are those collected by the Blisses. Greco-Roman coins, late Roman and early Byzantine bas-reliefs, Roman glass and bronzeware, and Egyptian fabrics are just a few of the highlights. In 1962 Robert Bliss donated his collection of pre-Columbian art, which required a specially designed wing to be added to the house. It includes masks and gold jewelry from Central America, and Aztec carvings.

Visitors to the gardens today can explore room after outdoor room of lovely landscaped spaces and flower gardens. There is a stunning walled rose garden, a fountain terrace, a wonderfully romantic 1930s-style swimming pool, and a formal boxwood garden, among others. Winding paths lead from one secret nook to another, lending a sense of mystery and wonder to the exploration.

EAT & DRINK

Dean & DeLuca
Famous gourmet deli, bistro, and store with imported foods.

📍 C4 🏠 3276 M St, NW
🌐 deandeluca.com

$$⑤

Pinstripes
Italian American bistro with ample room for bowling and bocce (a type of boules).

📍 C4 🏠 1064 Wisconsin Ave, NW
🌐 pinstripes.com

$$$

The Sovereign
Wonderful Belgian beers and food served in an attractive gastropub.

📍 C4 🏠 1206 Wisconsin Ave, NW 🌐 the sovereigndc.com

$$$

Blues Alley
Intimate jazz club with live performances and potent drinks.

📍 C4 🏠 1073 Wisconsin Ave, NW
🌐 bluesalley.com

$$⑤

6

Old Stone House

C4 **3051 M St, NW** **Foggy Bottom-GWU, then 15-min walk** **30, 32, 34, 36, 38** **11am–6pm daily; closed for repairs until Spring 2019** **nps.gov/olst**

Possibly the only building in Washington that predates the American Revolution, the Old Stone House was built in 1765 by Christopher Layman, and is now a welcome respite from the shops of busy M Street.

A legend that still persists about the Old Stone House is that it was the Suter's Tavern where Washington and Pierre L'Enfant made their plans for the city. However, most historians today believe that they met in a tavern located

elsewhere in Georgetown. Over the years, the building has housed a series of artisans, and in the 1950s it even served as offices for a used-car dealership. In 1960 the National Park Service restored it to its pre-Revolutionary War appearance. Today, park rangers give talks (noon–5pm) about what Georgetown would have been like in the Colonial period. The Old Stone House is technically the oldest house in DC, although the Lindens, now in Kalorama, was built in the mid-1750s in Massachusetts and later moved to Washington.

7

M Street

C4 **M St, NW** **Foggy Bottom-GWU, then 15-min walk** **30, 32, 34, 36, 38**

One of Georgetown's two main shopping streets,

Interior *(inset)* and exterior of the Old Stone House, possibly DC's oldest building

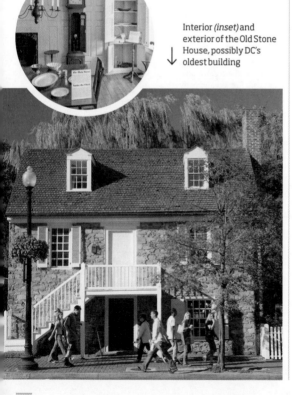

HIDDEN GEM
Exorcist Steps

Constructed in 1895, these steep stairs at 3600 Prospect Street, NW connect to M Street, NW. They featured in the 1973 horror film *The Exorcist*, when priest Father Karras tumbled down them headfirst.

M Street is also home to some of the most historic spots in the city. On the northeast corner of 30th and M streets, on the current site of a bank, stood Union Tavern. Built in 1796, it played host to, among others, presidents George Washington and John Adams, author Washington Irving, and Francis Scott Key, composer of "The Star-Spangled Banner." During the Civil War, the inn was turned into a temporary hospital where Louisa May Alcott, author of *Little Women*, nursed wounded soldiers.

William Thornton, architect of the US Capitol and Tudor Place *(p130)*, lived at 3219 M Street. On the south side of the street is Market House, which has been the location of Georgetown's market since 1751. A wood frame market house was built in 1796 and replaced by the current brick market in 1865. In the 1930s the market became an auto supply store, and in the 1990s the legendary deli and specialty shop Dean & DeLuca *(p125)* opened a branch here.

Today M Street and the adjacent blocks are home to fashionable stores and restaurants. Shop for alternative music at Hill & Dale Records and alternative clothing at Urban Outfitters, or visit stores such as Anthropologie, CB2, Banana Republic, and Starbucks. The fashionable Cady's Alley, at 3318 M Street, is a haven of trendy boutiques and high-end furnishing stores. Clyde's restaurant at 3236 is a Georgetown

↑ Georgetown's popular M Street, with a range of stores and restaurants

institution, famous for its happy hour. And Dean & DeLuca offers a shaded patio where you can sit, sip coffee, enjoy a pastry or fruit bowl and watch the people of Georgetown go by.

 8

Washington Post Office

⚲ C4 ⌂ 1215 31st St, NW Ⓜ Foggy Bottom-GWU, then 20-min walk 🚌 30, 32, 34, 36 ⏱ 9am-5pm Mon-Fri, 9am-2pm Sat

Built as a custom house in 1857, this still-functioning branch of the Washington Post Office is interesting both historically and architecturally. A custom house was a money-producing venture for the Federal government, and the US government's investment in such an expensive building is evidence of Georgetown's importance as a port for many years. Architect Ammi B. Young, who also designed the Vermont State Capitol building in 1832 and the Boston Custom House in 1837, was called to DC in 1852. While he designed several other Italianate buildings in the

capital, this post office is the finest example of his work. The granite custom house was converted to a post office when Georgetown's fortunes declined. The building underwent a renovation in 1997 that retained the integrity of Young's functional design.

In 2013, the post office was sold, and today, the space is used for private offices. A small post office station still exists, but the architecturally interesting interior is not accessible to the public.

⑨

N Street

⚲ C4 ⌂ N St, NW Ⓜ Foggy Bottom-GWU, then 15-min walk 🚌 30, 32, 34, 36

N Street is a collection of 18th-century American Federal row houses. This style was favored by leaders of the new nation as being of a more refined design than the earlier Georgian architecture. At the corner of 30th and N streets is the Laird-Dunlop House. Today it is owned by Sally Quinn, the widow of Benjamin Bradlee, the former editor of the *Washington Post*. An excellent example of a Federal house is the Riggs-Riley House at 3038 N Street, once owned by diplomats and socialites Averill and Pamela Harriman. At 3041–3045 is Wheatley Row, houses built above street level with large windows, offering maximum light but also maximum privacy. The house at 3307 is where the Kennedys lived before moving to the White House.

1770
—
The oldest surviving house on N Street, 3033, was built by mayor Thomas Beall.

SHOP

Alice + Olivia
Hip, upscale boutique with chic women's fashions and accessories for all occasions.
⚲ B4 ⌂ 3303 M St, NW 🖥 aliceandolivia.com

Billy Reid
Antique-filled store showcasing the Alabama-based designer's vintage rock chic.
⚲ C4 ⌂ 3211 M St, NW 🖥 billyreid.com

Frank Milwee
Browse a quality selection of antiques, with silver, home decor, and unusual items at this M Street store. Don't miss the corkscrews.
⚲ C4 ⌂ 2912 M St, NW ☏ (202) 333-4811

Hu's Wear and Hu's Shoes
Local style guru Marlene Hu Aldaba curates her two shops with stylish and bold fashion pieces, plus an on-trend selection of handbags and accessories.
⚲ C4; D4 ⌂ Hu's Wear: 2906 M St, NW; Hu's Shoes: 3005 M St, NW 🖥 husonline.com

Cady's Alley
An irresistible cluster of high-end fashion, jewelry, design, and home furnishing shops located on the south side of M Street.
⚲ B4 ⌂ 3314 M St, NW 🖥 cadysalley.com

Colorful Colonial houses in Georgetown

10

Tudor Place

📍C3 🏠1664 31st St, NW
Ⓜ Dupont Circle, Foggy
Bottom-GWU, then bus
🕐10am-4pm Tue-Sat,
noon-4pm Sun ⓧCheck
website ⓦtudorplace.org

The manor house and large gardens of this Georgetown estate, designed by British-American physician, inventor, painter, and architect William Thornton (1759–1828), who also designed the Capitol, offer a unique glimpse into a bygone era.

Martha Washington, the wife of George Washington and America's first First Lady, gave $8,000 to her granddaughter, Martha Custis Peter, and her granddaughter's husband, Thomas Peter. With the money, they purchased 8 acres (3.2 ha) and commissioned Thornton to design a grand house. Six generations of the Peters family lived here from 1805 to 1984. It is something of a mystery as to why this stuccoed, two-story Georgian structure with a "temple" porch is called Tudor Place, but it was perhaps illustrative of the English sympathies held by the family at that time. The furniture, silver, china, and portraits in Tudor Place provide a glimpse into American social and cultural history; some of the pieces on display come from Mount Vernon *(p162)*.

Outside, 5.5 acres (2.2 ha) of formal gardens and picturesque woodland spaces can be explored along pretty stone paths.

11

Georgetown University

📍B4 🏠37th & O Sts, NW
Ⓜ Rosslyn, then bus
ⓦgeorgetown.edu

Georgetown University was the first Catholic college to be established in America. Founded in 1789 by John Carroll, and affiliated with the Jesuit Order, the university now attracts students of all faiths from more than 100 countries around the world.

The oldest building on the campus is the Old North Building, completed in 1872. However, the most recognizable structure is the Healy Building, a Germanic design topped by a fanciful spiral. The university's most famous graduate is former US president Bill Clinton.

INSIDER TIP
Kayak the Potomac

Rent kayaks, canoes, or sculls at the Thompson Boat Center at 2900 Virginia Avenue, NW and paddle the gentle waters past Roosevelt Island, Kennedy Center, the Lincoln Memorial, and the Georgetown Waterfront Park.

12

Oak Hill Cemetery

📍D3 🏠3001 R St, NW
Ⓜ Dupont Circle, then bus
🕐9am-4:30pm Mon-Fri,
11am-4pm Sat, 1-4pm Sun
ⓧFederal hols ⓦoakhill
cemeterydc.org

Washingtonian banker, art collector, and philanthropist William Wilson Corcoran bought the land on which Congress established the Oak Hill Cemetery in 1849. Today, about 18,000 graves cover this 25-acre (10-ha) site, which is planted with huge oak trees. Members of some of the city's most prominent families are buried here, their names featured throughout its history,

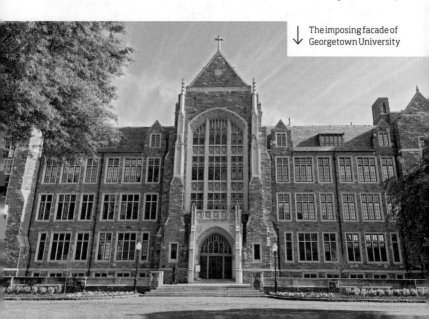

↓ The imposing facade of Georgetown University

↑ Georgetown Waterfront Park, a peaceful spot to take a break

including Magruder, Thomas, Beall, and Marbury. Lincoln's son William is also buried here.

At the cemetery's entrance is an Italianate gatehouse that is still used as the superintendent's lodge and office. Northeast of it is the Spencer family monument, designed by Louis Comfort Tiffany. The granite low-relief of an angel is signed by Tiffany.

Another notable monument is the Van Ness mausoleum, built in 1833 for the wife of John Peter Van Ness, mayor of Washington. Designed by George Hadfield, it is said to be a copy of the Temple of Vesta in Rome.

Also worth visiting is the Gothic chapel designed by James Renwick and located on the cemetery's highest ridge, near the intersection of 29th and R streets, NW. Nearby is the grave of John Howard Payne, composer of the well-loved song "Home, Sweet Home," who died in 1852. The bust atop Payne's monument was originally sculpted with a full beard, but Corcoran asked a stonemason to "shave the statue" and it now appears clean shaven.

> **The bust atop Payne's monument was originally sculpted with a full beard, but Corcoran asked a stonemason to "shave the statue" and it now appears clean shaven.**

13

Georgetown Waterfront Park

📍 C5 🏠 Bottom of Wisconsin Ave Ⓜ Foggy Bottom-GWU, then 15-min walk 🌐 georgetown waterfrontpark.org

This lovely riverfront park adjacent to Washington Harbour offers locals and visitors alike a place to enjoy the surprising beauty of the Potomac River. Shaded lawns offer respite in summer, and inviting benches offer wonderful views of the park and river. There is also a great view downriver to the Kennedy Center. Wide walking paths extend north to Georgetown and south to East Potomac Park along the popular Capital Crescent Trail. Overlooks along the riverfront are decorated with carved panels that tell the story of the area's early days as a busy port. There is also a labyrinth that is popular with kids and those seeking serenity. A stream gauge at the western end of the park lets visitors check the height of the river water.

14

Mount Zion Church

📍 D4 🏠 1334 29th St, NW Ⓜ Foggy Bottom-GWU, Dupont Circle, then bus 🌐 mtzionumcdc.org

This church is thought to have had the first black congregation in DC. The original church, at 27th and P streets, was a "station" on the city's original Underground Railroad, offering shelter for runaway slaves on their journey north to freedom. The present redbrick building was completed in 1884 after the first church burned down. Mount Zion Cemetery, the oldest black burial ground in the city, is nearby, in the middle of the 2500 block of Q Street.

SOUTH OF THE MALL

A decade ago, this part of the city was made up of ageing warehouses, government buildings, and third-rate office complexes that were a wasteland for visitors. A radical multi-billion-dollar makeover has transformed the area into a shiny riverfront playground for dining, shopping, and entertainment in the city. Cornerstones of the region are the Nationals Park and the phenomenal District Wharf development, a mile-long (1.5-km) stretch of gleaming glass and steel high-rises offering some of DC's hottest new restaurants, waterfront parks, live music venues, and several ways to get out on the river for a good time. There is one thing that did not change, except for the better: the old fish market where traditional, open-air, family-run stalls and restaurants offer superfresh seafood raw or cooked to order.

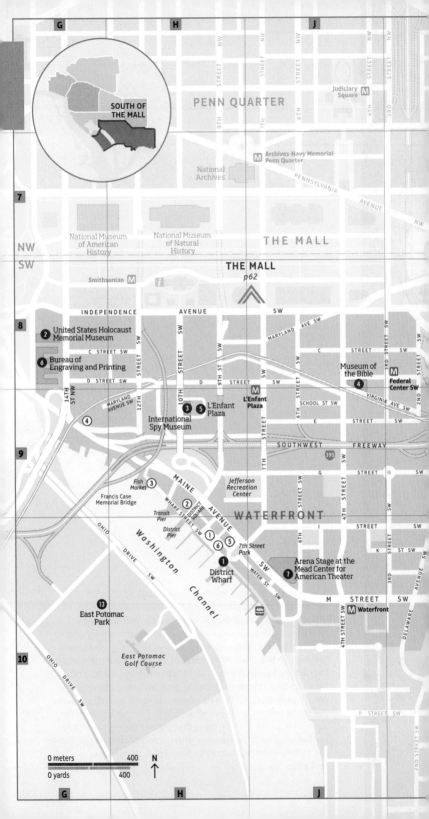

SOUTH OF THE MALL

Must Sees

❶ District Wharf

❷ United States Holocaust Memorial Museum

❸ International Spy Museum

Experience More

❹ Museum of the Bible

❺ L'Enfant Plaza

❻ Bureau of Engraving and Printing

❼ Arena Stage at the Mead Center for American Theater

❽ Navy Yard Park

❾ Nationals Park

❿ National Museum of the US Navy

⓫ Cold War Gallery

⓬ Blind Whino SW Arts Club

⓭ East Potomac Park

Eat

① Del Mar de Fabio Trabocchi

② Requin

③ Jessie Taylor Seafood

④ Muze

Stay

⑤ Canopy by Hilton

⑥ Hyatt House Washington DC/ The Wharf

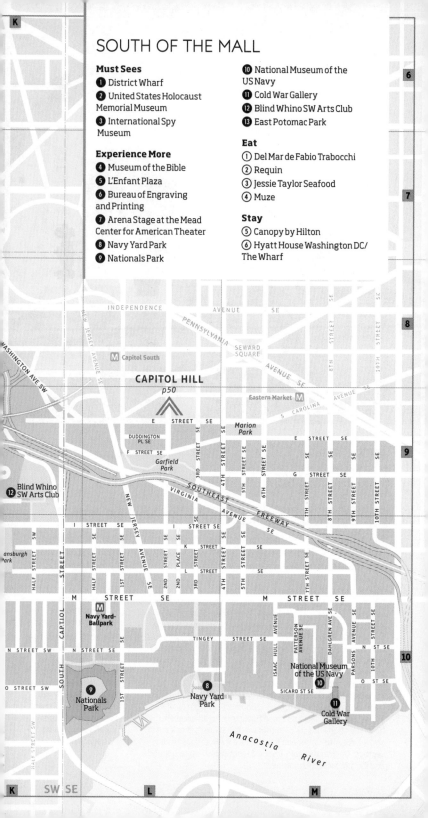

Did You Know?

The Wharf Jitney offers a free ride across the Washington Channel to East Potomac Park.

1 🍽 💻 🛍

DISTRICT WHARF

📍 H10 🏛 Maine Ave, SW between Market Sq & 7th St, SW Ⓜ Waterfront, L'Enfant Plaza 🚌 52, 74 🕐 Daily 🌐 wharfdc.com

This neighborhood was filled with crumbling government and office buildings and military warehouses only a few years ago. Today, an expensive facelift has resulted in this exciting waterside development along Washington Channel.

On the waterfront, the largest pier is home to the traditional Maine Avenue Fish Market, where you can select and take home ultrafresh seafood, or have it cooked to order to eat on-site. Other piers include Transit Pier, where live concerts take place and water taxis ply their trade, and District Pier, dedicated to a wide range of entertainment and recreation. Several park-like open areas offer shaded spots to sit and enjoy great views of the bustling marinas, and there are enough inviting restaurants and trendy shops to keep visitors entertained for hours. Pop into A Beautiful Closet for home decor and gifts, the Martha Spak Gallery for fine contemporary art from local artists, or the Politics and Prose bookstore for an excellent book selection and lots of author readings. Take a break at Kith and Kin for Afro-Caribbean food, Kaliwa for Southeast Asian seafood, Del Mar de Fabio Trabocchi for Spanish-style seafood, and Requin for French cuisine.

 PICTURE PERFECT
Potomac Pictures

The water taxi running between Washington Harbor, Georgetown, and National Harbor provides splendid photo opportunities. Try to catch it around sunset for the best pictures of the city skyline and the Potomac River.

EAT

Del Mar de Fabio Trabocchi
Superfresh seafood with Spanish flavors.

🔢H10 🏠791 Wharf St, SW 🌐delmardc.com

$$$

Requin
Contemporary French place with great views.

🔢H9 🏠100 District Sq, SW 🌐requinbymic.com

$$$

Jessie Taylor Seafood
Freshly cooked seafood beside the Wharf.

🔢H9 🏠1100 Maine Ave 🌐jessietaylor seafood.com

$$$

↑ Washington's gleaming waterfront development at District Wharf

1 Opened in 1805, the Maine Avenue Fish Market is one of the country's oldest continually operating fish markets, with stalwarts such as Jessie Taylor Seafood.

2 Seafood dishes are a popular choice at District Wharf.

3 Waterfront Park offers visitors lovely views of the busy marinas, the Washington Channel, and the serene Potomac River.

6,000,000
———
Jews and millions of others were killed by the Nazi government as part of the Final Solution.

↑ The three-story "Tower of Faces," devoted to the Jewish community of Eišiškės, Lithuania

②

UNITED STATES HOLOCAUST MEMORIAL MUSEUM

📍 G8 🏠 100 Raoul Wallenburg Place, SW Ⓜ Smithsonian 🚌 13 (Pentagon shuttle)
🕙 10am–5:20pm daily 🚫 Yom Kippur, Dec 25 🌐 ushmm.org

Solemn and respectful yet engrossing and informative, the challenging Holocaust Museum is a study center for issues relating to the Holocaust as well as a national memorial for the millions murdered by the Nazi government during World War II.

The museum, opened in 1993, bears witness to the systematic persecution and murder in Europe of millions of Jews and others deemed undesirable by the Third Reich, including political objectors, intellectuals, gypsies, homosexuals, and the disabled. The space ranges from the intentionally claustrophobic to the soaringly majestic. About 2,500 photographs, 1,000 artifacts, 53 video monitors, and 30 interactive stations containing graphic and emotionally disturbing images of violence grimly detail the surveillance and loss of individual rights, forcing visitors to confront the horror of the Holocaust. While "Daniel's Story" is aimed at children of eight years and up, the permanent exhibition is not recommended for those under 12 years. Free timed passes are needed from March to August; same-day walk-up passes are available alongside online advance and same-day passes.

↑ The museum building, designed to reference Holocaust sites via its abstract architectural forms

GALLERY GUIDE

The Holocaust Museum is meant to be an immersive experience. Starting from the top, footage, artifacts, photographs, and survivor testimonies can be seen from the fourth to the second floors. The first floor has the Hall of Witness and "Daniel's Story," and the Concourse has the Children's Tile Wall.

↑ The "Final Solution" exhibit, including a boxcar used to carry prisoners to concentration camps

3 ⬡ ⬡ ⬡ ⬡

INTERNATIONAL SPY MUSEUM

📍H9 🏠700 L'Enfant Plaza, SW Ⓜ️L'Enfant Plaza 🕐Times vary, check website 🚫Jan 1, Thanksgiving, Dec 25 🌐spymuseum.org

This fascinating museum shows the world of spycraft and how intelligence gathering and espionage shape the world we live in. The one-of-a-kind, world-class collection of spy gadgets and memorabilia enhance the fascinating museum experience, which assumes that each guest is a spy-in-training.

Becoming an effective spy requires many skills and tools, and "School for Spies" not only explains them but also provides insights into how and why people become spies. "Spies Among Us" has stories of real-life spies and interactive codebreaking exhibits. The celebrity spies exhibit includes actress Marlene Dietrich and director John Ford, while "The Secret History of History" tells tales of espionage from biblical times to the early 20th century. Visitors' newfound skills can be put into practice by joining the immersive "Operation Spy" program. In 2019, the museum relocated to L'Enfant Plaza, where expansive new facilities include a lecture theater and a vast rooftop terrace.

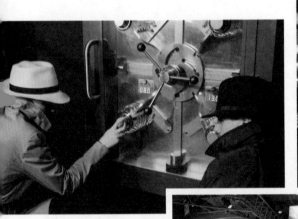

↑ Visitors trying out code-breaking exhibits in "Spies Among Us"

Did You Know?

George Washington's spy code name was 711 and Congress paid him $17,000 for espionage expenses.

↑ "School for Spies," offering insights and tips of the trade

c 1800 BC	1778	1950–80	2018
△ A clay tablet from Babylonian king Hammurabi records information about his spies - the oldest record of espionage.	△ Benjamin Franklin becomes the United States ambassador to France; in fact, he is one of the country's earliest spies.	△ The Cold War triggers a renaissance in spy-craft, with microdot cameras creating images the size of a newspaper punctuation mark.	△ Modern tech turns everyone into a spy: tiny drones built using standard electronics can eavesdrop on cell phone conversations.

↑ James Bond's Aston Martin from *Goldfinger* (1964), inspiration for real-life spy vehicles

One of the immersive exhibits at the massive Museum of the Bible ↑

EXPERIENCE MORE

4
Museum of the Bible

📍J8 ⬛400 4th St, SW Ⓜ L'Enfant Plaza 🕐Apr-Jun: 10am-6pm daily; Jul-Mar: 10am-5pm daily 🚫Jan 1, Thanksgiving, Dec 25 🌐museumofthebible.org

Containing what may well be the world's largest collection of Bibles and biblical artifacts, the Bible Museum is one of Washington's major attractions. It fills six floors of a massive building that was the 1923 Terminal Refrigerating and Warehousing Company before it had an estimated $400-million makeover.

The aim of the museum is to document the history and impact of the Bible, as well as relate the stories within it. Each floor has a theme. The first floor features a collection of art and printed works from the Vatican museums. The second floor traces the impact of the Bible from ancient to modern times. The third floor focuses on relating the stories

of the Hebrew Bible and Nazareth in the era of Jesus. The fourth floor relates the history of the Bible, and the fifth floor has a remarkable collection of antiquities from ancient Israel. And on the sixth floor is chef Todd Gray's casual restaurant, Manna, as well as an atrium that offers one of the most breathtaking views of Washington.

5
L'Enfant Plaza

📍H9 ⬛Between L'Enfant Plaza SW & 7th St, SW Ⓜ L'Enfant Plaza Ⓜ lenfantplaza.com

Newly renovated and expanded, the plaza is at the hub of the rapidly upscaling Southwest DC area. An underground mall with over 40 shops and food-court eateries makes this one of the closest places to the Mall to find fast, affordable food. An outdoor entertainment area offers free summer concerts.

6
Bureau of Engraving and Printing

📍G8 ⬛14th & C Sts, SW Ⓜ Smithsonian 🕐8:30am-2:45pm Mon-Fri (to 6pm Mar-Aug) 🚫Week after Christmas, Federal hols 🌐moneyfactory.gov

Until 1863, individual banks were responsible for printing American money. A shortage of coins and the need to finance the Civil War led to the production of standardized banknotes, and the Bureau of

---

💬 INSIDER TIP
Water Taxis

Water taxis run by the Potomac Riverboat Company (potomacriverboatco.com) from Old Town Alexandria, the National Harbor, and Georgetown to the Wharf offer spectacular views of the Potomac.

7

Arena Stage at the Mead Center for American Theater

📍 J10 📌 1101 6th St SW
Ⓜ Waterfront 🌐 arena
stage.org

Founded in 1950, the Arena Stage was one of the first non-profit theaters in the US, and is dedicated to promoting American plays and play-wrights. The award-winning theater has a long history of producing not only classic works, but new, cutting-edge works by emerging writers. In 1967 the arena became the first regional theater to pro-duce a play that went on to Broadway – Howard Sackler's *The Great White Hope*, which won the best play Tony in 1969.

8

Navy Yard Park

📍 L10 📌 355 Water St, SE
Ⓜ Navy Yard-Ballpark
🌐 capitolriverfront.org/
yards-park

Relatively unknown to visitors, this lovely public space that stretches along the banks of the Anacostia River is quickly becoming a favorite with DC residents. The centerpiece of

---

EAT

Muze

The Mandarin Oriental hotel's waterfront eatery serves modern American food with an Asian twist.

📍 G9 📌 1330 Maryland Ave, SW
🌐 mandarinoriental.
com/washington/
national-mall

$$$

Engraving and Printing was founded. Initially housed in the Treasury Building (p112), it was moved to its present location in 1914. It prints over $140 billion a year, as well as stamps, Federal documents, and White House invitations. The 40-minute tour includes a short film, and a walk through the building to view the printing processes. Also on display are bills that are out of circulation, counterfeit money, and a special $100,000 bill.

this family-oriented park is a large wading pool that children and adults are encouraged to splash about in. The dancing fountains are a water art feature that visi-tors can run through – a very popular attraction on hot summer days. Green lawns make a great place for picnics, and there are tree-shaded benches and a pleasant waterfront walkway. Buildings surrounding the park house an array of fine and fast-food restaurants. Free movies and concerts are put on during the summer, and the park plays host to the DC Jazz Festival.

↓ A cooling water feature at the Navy Yard Park

STAY

Canopy by Hilton

This nautical-themed boutique hotel with a rooftop bar and river views offers evening tastings of local wines, brews, or spirits.

📍H10 🏠975 7th St, SW 🌐canopy3.hilton.com

$$$

Hyatt House Washington DC/ The Wharf

Extended stay hotel with expansive river views. Some rooms have a kitchenette and living area. There's also a fitness room, seasonal outdoor swimming pool, and complimentary breakfast.

📍H10 🏠725 Wharf St, SW 🌐hyatt.com

$$$

Nationals Park

📍L10 🏠1500 S Capitol St, SE Ⓜ Navy Yard-Ballpark, Capitol South 🌐mlb.com/nationals/ballpark

Another popular venue at the expanding Southwest Waterfront, the $784-million Nationals Park was opened to rave reviews in 2008. President George W. Bush threw the ceremonial first pitch. The stadium has a seating capacity of 41,339, as well as 79 suites on three levels, and is the first LEED-certified green major league stadium in the United States. From the upper stands visitors can take in a view stretching to the Washington Monument and the US Capitol. In honor

of the Naval Yards in the surrounding area, since 2011 the stadium has sounded a submarine "dive" klaxon when the Nationals baseball team score a home run. Several iconic city restaurants operate food concessions in the park, including Ben's Chili Bowl.

National Museum of the US Navy

📍M10 🏠736 Sicard St, SE, Building 76 Ⓜ Navy Yard-Ballpark, Eastern Market 🕐9am-5pm Mon-Sat (from noon Tue, 10am Sat); valid photo ID or advance permission needed, see website 🌐history.navy.mil/nmusn

This large museum should be better known, as it contains a wealth of impressive exhibits tracing the history of the US Navy from the Revolutionary War to modern times. Themes include the role of the navy in the Civil War, the shift from wood to steel, and the rise of the Great White Fleet, among others. A large exhibit focuses on deep-sea exploration and features the bathyscaphe (manned submersible) *Trieste*, which made a record dive to 35,797 ft (10,910 m) in the Mariana Trench in 1960. The exhibit also features a full-size replica of the deep sea submersible *Alvin* (DSV-2). The exhibit "The Forgotten Wars of the 19th Century" displays

a replica of the gun deck of the famous USS *Constitution*, the wooden-hulled, three-masted frigate named by George Washington after the Constitution of the new United States and affectionately known as Old Ironsides.

Cold War Gallery

📍M10 🏠736 Sicard St, SE, Building 70 Ⓜ Navy Yard-Ballpark, Eastern Market 🕐9am-4:30pm Mon-Fri; valid photo ID or advance permission needed, see website 🌐history.navy.mil/nmusn

Located next door to the Navy Museum, this large museum defines the Cold War and tells the story of the US Navy's role

←

Nautical exhibits on display at the National Museum of the US Navy

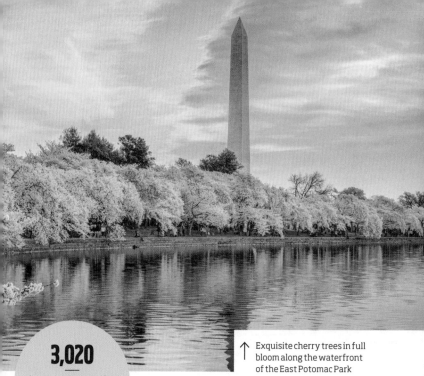

3,020
—
cherry trees were gifted to the city by Japan in 1912 and planted in this area by 1920.

↑ Exquisite cherry trees in full bloom along the waterfront of the East Potomac Park

in fighting it. Just inside the entrance of the museum is a full-size Trident C-4 missile. To put visitors in the mood for the theme of the museum, one of the first exhibits they experience is the "Ready Room," a reproduction of a real ready room, where pilots would get their orders just before flying out to undertake top secret intelligence missions. Other exhibits in the museum cover the role the United States played in the Korean and Vietnam wars, nuclear-era technology, and the gathering of intelligence with submarines, high altitude aircraft, and satellites. The "Covert Submarine Operations" exhibit has on display a full nuclear submarine command center from the USS *Trepang*, a Sturgeon-class attack submarine that was in service from 1970 to 1999.

 Blind Whino SW Arts Club

📍K9 🏠700 Delaware Ave, SW Ⓜ Waterfront 🕐5-8pm Wed; noon-5pm Sat & Sun (Art Annex) 🌐swarts club.org

It is hard not to fall in love at first sight with this dazzlingly painted, 1886 Baptist church, now a fascinating center for the presentation and promotion of art. It has a 15,000-sq-ft (1,394-m) mural-covered interior, created as a public gathering and performance space. The club is dedicated to providing a dynamic environment for concerts and performances of all types, and where people of all ages can celebrate and create art. The Art Annex, a gallery open to the public on weekends, hosts shows of regionally and nationally known artists. Outside, there are organic gardens that create produce for local shops and restaurants.

 East Potomac Park

📍H10 🏠Ohio Dr, SW Ⓜ Waterfront

This low-key park occupies a long peninsula that extends south of the Tidal Basin and separates the Washington Channel from the Potomac River. A leafy green expanse, with a loop road and broad lawns, it is a favorite with joggers, cyclists, and anyone who wants to experience one of the quieter places along the riverfront. The park offers several sports venues – a golf course, swimming pool, soccer fields, and tennis courts – but its most popular feature is the concrete walkway that follows the waterfront on both sides of the peninsula. Anyone who wants a long stroll can wend their way past the ever-present cadres of rail-leaning fishermen and enjoy the views of glittering District Wharf on one side and the verdant western shore of the river on the other.

NORTHWEST

A remarkable area with two distinctly different personalities, the Northwest is a collection of old and new neighborhoods. Kalorama, lying northwest of L'Enfant's original city limits, remained a mainly rural area until the end of the 19th century, when Congress ordered the city plan to be extended outwards. Today, Kalorama and Embassy Row are highly walkable areas, with lovely tree-shaded sidewalks and a century's worth of elegant mansions lining the streets, many containing embassies from around the world. Dupont Circle and the ethnically diverse Adams-Morgan are the area's established cool neighborhoods where you will find bookstores, wine shops, restaurants, and nightlife. Farther east, the culturally rich and varied Shaw neighborhood had its origins in settlements set up in the city's rural outskirts by newly freed slaves coming to the north. It is now one of the city's trendiest zones, with cutting-edge restaurants vying for space with gastropubs and mezcal bars. Here too, are the historic Howard and Lincoln theaters, once famous stages in the "Black Broadway." Now renovated, they present a full schedule of plays and concerts with a strong theme of diversity.

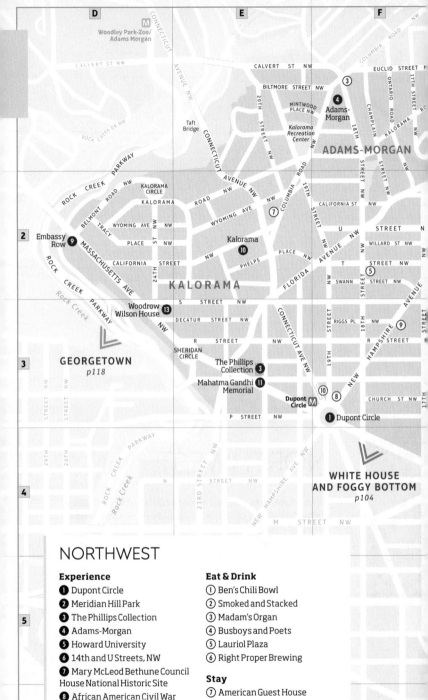

NORTHWEST

EXPERIENCE

① Dupont Circle

⊘ F3 Ⓜ Dupont Circle

This area to the north of the White House gets its name from the park-like Dupont traffic circle and the lovely Francis Dupont Memorial Fountain, named for a naval Civil War hero. In the early 20th century the Dupont Circle area was a place of grand mansions, but over the years its fortunes declined. Then, in the 1970s, Washingtonians began to buy and restore the decaying old buildings. The district is now one of the liveliest and most sophisticated in DC, with art galleries, bars, restaurants, and bookstores. The present marble fountain, constructed

in 1921, has four figures – representing the sea, the wind, the stars, and the navigational arts – supporting a marble basin. The park around the fountain draws a cross section of the community – chess players engrossed in their games, cyclists pausing at the fountain, picnickers, and tourists taking a break.

---

② Meridian Hill Park

**⊘ G1 ☐ 16th & W Sts, NW
Ⓜ U Street/African-Amer Civil War Memorial/Cardozo
ⓦ nps.gov/places/meridian-hill-park.htm**

In 1819, John Porter built an ornate mansion on Meridian Hill, so named because it was on the exact longitude of the original DC milestone marker set in April 1791. The mansion was later the home of outgoing president John Quincy Adams. Just before the Civil War, a pleasure park was developed on the hill, which later became a bivouac area for Union soldiers during the war. Begun in 1914, the ornate,

Italianate-style park of today has spreading shade trees, grassy expanses, wide stone stairways, and hilltop terraces with views across the park. The centerpiece is a spectacular fountain that cascades down the hillside through 13 basins. The park's Joan of Arc statue is the city's only equestrian statue of a woman. The popular park can get busy, especially in summer when the grounds are occupied by families enjoying picnics.

---

③   The Phillips Collection

**⊘ E3 ☐ 1600 21st St at Q St, NW Ⓜ Dupont Circle
☐ 10am–5pm Tue–Sat (to 8:30pm Thu), noon–6:30pm Sun ☐ Jan 1, Jul 4, Thanksgiving, Dec 25, Federal hols ⓦ phillipscollection.org**

This is one of the world's finest collections of Impressionist and contemporary art, and the first museum devoted to modern art in the US. It was founded in 1917 by Duncan and Marjorie Phillips, who opened part of their home as the Phillips Memorial Gallery.

The couple spent their time traveling and adding to their already extensive collection. During the 1920s they acquired some of the most important modern European paintings, including *The Luncheon of the Boating Party* (1881) by Renoir.

Their elegant 1897 Georgian-Revival home is now the permanent gallery for the Phillips Collection, and provides an intimate space for appreciating the artworks. The collection has over 43,000

←
The Francis Dupont Memorial Fountain at Dupont Circle

↑ Colorful restaurants, cafés, and stores in the vibrant Adams-Morgan neighborhood

pieces of 19th-, 20th-, and 21st-century American and European art. There is a wonderful group of Impressionist and Post-Impressionist works: *Dancers at the Barre* by Degas, *Self-Portrait* by Cézanne, and *Entrance to the Public Gardens in Arles* by Van Gogh are just three examples. The museum has one of the world's largest collections of works by French artist Pierre Bonnard, including *The Open Window* (1921), plus several large Rothko pieces.

On the first Thursday of each month the museum hosts "Phillips after 5," evenings of gallery talks and live music. On Sunday afternoons from September through May, a series of concerts are staged in the gallery's Music Room.

Adams-Morgan

⚲ F1 **⌂ North of Dupont Circle, east of Rock Creek Park, and south of Mount Pleasant** **Ⓜ Dupont Circle, Woodley Park-Zoo/Adams Morgan**

Packed with cafés, bookstores, clubs, and galleries, Adams-Morgan was one of the city's first racially and ethnically diverse neighborhoods and is a vibrant mix of gay and straight African, Hispanic, and Caribbean immigrants and white urban pioneers. People are attracted by the district's lively streets and its beautiful, and relatively affordable, early 20th-century houses and apartments. The area has a thriving music scene and a wide variety of world cuisines can be found in the restaurants along 18th Street and Columbia Road. This cultural diversity is celebrated in September each year with food, music, and dance at the Adams-Morgan Day Festival.

EAT & DRINK

Ben's Chili Bowl
Legendary 1950s-style diner serving all the city's movers and shakers.

⚲ H2 **⌂ 1213 U St, NW**
ⓦ benschilibowl.com

Smoked and Stacked
Hearty sandwiches for breakfast and home-cured pastrami and smoked meats for lunch.

⚲ H4 **⌂ 1239 9th St, NW**
ⓦ smokedandstacked.com

Madam's Organ
Live music nightly at this popular blues bar and soul food restaurant.

⚲ F1 **⌂ 2461 18th St, NW**
ⓦ madamsorgan.com

Busboys and Poets
Excellent vegetarian, vegan, and meat entrees served 24 hours daily.

⚲ G2 **⌂ 2021 14th St, NW**
ⓦ busboysandpoets.com

Lauriol Plaza
Tex-Mex and Latin American food served in a vibrant urban setting.

⚲ F2 **⌂ 1835 18th St, NW**
ⓦ lauriolplaza.com

Right Proper Brewing
Brewpub with local beers and casual Southern comfort food from the kitchen.

⚲ J2 **⌂ 624 T St, NW**
Ⓓ D only Mon–Thu
ⓦ rightproperbrewing.com

The intersection of 14th and U streets, one of the liveliest districts in the city ↑

5

Howard University

📍 J2 📌 2400 6th St, NW
Ⓜ Shaw-Howard
University 🌐 howard.edu

The first Congregational Society of Washington set up a seminary in 1866 for the education of African-Americans. The concept expanded to include a university, and within two years the Colleges of Liberal Arts and Medicine of Howard University were founded, named for General Oliver O. Howard (1830–1909), an abolitionist and Civil War hero who later became a commissioner of the Freedman's Bureau. The impetus was the arrival of newly freed men coming to the North seeking education to improve their lives. The university's charter was enacted by Congress and approved by President Andrew Jackson.

Famous graduates include Thurgood Marshall, the first African-American Supreme Court Justice, historian Carter Woodson, writers Ta-Nehisi Coates and Toni Morrison, actor and writer Ossie Davis, civil rights activist Stokely Carmichael, and rapper and music mogul Sean Combs, better known as Puff Daddy.

6 🍴 🖥 🛍

14th and U Streets, NW

📍 G2 Ⓜ U Street/African-Amer Civil War Memorial/Cardozo

The intersection of 14th and U streets, NW is the gateway to one of Washington's most vibrant neighborhoods. Until the middle of the 20th century, U Street, once known as the "Black Broadway," hosted prominent African-American entertainers, including Duke Ellington and Pearl Bailey. They performed at the Lincoln and Howard theaters as well as in many nightclubs. 14th Street, known as Automobile Row, was lined with posh car showrooms. But in 1968 both 14th and U streets burned in the riots that ensued after the assassination of Dr. Martin Luther King. Businesses fled the area and for decades it was left to drug trafficking and crime. Well-respected local company Studio Theatre bought a derelict car showroom in 1997 and built a state-of-the-art performance space. High-end apartments, restaurants, music venues, and bars followed. Today, the area, known as the U Street

---

THE SHAW NEIGHBOURHOOD

This neighborhood is named for Union Colonel Robert Gould Shaw, the white commander of an all-black regiment from Massachusetts. He supported his men in their struggle to attain the same rights as white soldiers. Until the 1960s, U Street was home to flourishing African-American businesses and organizations. Thriving theaters, such as the Howard and the Lincoln, attracted top-name artists, and Howard University was the center of intellectual life for black students. The 1968 riots, sparked by the assassination of Dr. Martin Luther King, Jr., wiped out much of Shaw's business district, and many thought the area could never be revived. However, the restoration of the Lincoln, the renewal of the business district, and an influx of buyers renovating historic houses have all contributed to the rejuvenation, with trendy bars, clubs, and stores opening on U Street.

Corridor, is a thriving spot for late-night entertainment. Of note is the famous Ben's Chili Bowl (p151), a landmark restaurant established in 1958.

7

Mary McLeod Bethune Council House National Historic Site

⚐ G4 **⌂** 1318 Vermont Ave, NW **Ⓜ** McPherson Square, Mt Vernon Sq/7th St-Convention Center **🕐** 9am–5pm daily **🚫** Jan 1, Thanksgiving, Dec 25 **🌐** nps.gov/mamc

Born in 1875 to two former slaves, Mary McLeod Bethune was an educator and civil and women's rights activist. In 1904 she founded the Daytona Literary and Industrial School for Negro Girls, a college for impoverished black women in Florida. Renamed the Bethune-Cookman College in 1931, it achieved university status in 2007.

In the 1930s, Franklin D. Roosevelt asked Bethune to be his special advisor on racial affairs, and she later became director of the Division of Negro Affairs in the National Youth Administration. As part of President Roosevelt's cabinet, she was the first black woman to obtain a high position in the US government.

Bethune went on to found the National Council of Negro Women, which gives voice to the concerns of black women. It grew to have a membership of 10,000, and this house was bought by Bethune and the council as its headquarters. It was not until November 1979, 24 years after Bethune's death, that the house was opened to the public, with photographs, manuscripts, and other artifacts from her life on display. In 1982 the house was declared a National Historic Site and was bought by the National Park Service.

8

African American Civil War Memorial and Museum

⚐ H2 **⌂** Museum: 1925 Vermont Ave, NW; memorial: 10th & U Sts, NW **Ⓜ** U Street/African-Amer Civil War Memorial/Cardozo **🕐** 10am–6:30pm Tue-Fri, 10am–4pm Sat, noon–4pm Sun **🌐** afroamcivilwar.org

Opened in January 1999, the African American Civil War Museum uses photographs, documents, and audiovisual equipment to tell the story of African-Americans' long struggle for freedom. The museum's permanent exhibition is entitled "Slavery to Freedom: Civil War to Civil Rights." Interactive kiosks bring together historic documents, photographs, and music in a powerful and evocative way. There is also a service for anyone interested in tracing relatives who may have served with United States Colored Troops during the Civil War.

At the center of a paved plaza nearby is the *Spirit of Freedom*, a sculpture by Ed Hamilton, which was unveiled on July 18, 1998. It is the first major art piece by a black sculptor on Federal land in the District of Columbia. Standing 10 ft (3 m) tall, the memorial features black soldiers and a sailor poised to leave home.

←

Ed Hamilton's *Spirit of Freedom* sculpture at the African American Civil War Memorial

STAY

American Guest House

Classic 1898 row house B&B in Kalorama. Its 12 guest rooms, elegantly furnished with antiques, have modern amenities. A lavish breakfast is included.

⚐ E2 **⌂** 2005 Columbia Rd, NW **🌐** americanguesthouse.com

$$$

The Dupont Circle Hotel

Located on Dupont Circle with easy access to vibrant nightlife and hip restaurants. The guest rooms are modern, and some suites have balconies with city views.

⚐ F3 **⌂** 1500 New Hampshire Ave, NW **🌐** doylecollection.com/hotels/the-dupont-circle-hotel

$$$

Kimpton Carlyle Hotel

Boutique hotel with Art Deco styling just three blocks from Dupont Circle. Fine dining at the in-house Riggsby restaurant.

⚐ F3 **⌂** 1731 New Hampshire Ave, NW **🌐** carlylehoteldc.com

$$$

Vibrant nightlife on U Street in Washington's Northwest district

The Greek Embassy on Embassy Row, Kalorama

apartment buildings are on Connecticut Avenue, south of the Taft Bridge that crosses Rock Creek Park. Most notable are the Georgian Revival-style apartments at number 2126, the Beaux Arts-inspired building at 1914, and the Spanish Colonial-style apartments at 2311. Also worth a look is the Tudor-style building at 2221 Kalorama Road.

Embassy Row

D2 **Massachusetts Ave, NW** **M** **Dupont Circle**

Stretching from Scott Circle toward Observatory Circle, Embassy Row developed during the Depression when many of the city's wealthy families were forced to sell their mansions to diplomats, who bought them for foreign missions. Since then, many more embassies have been built, often in the vernacular style of their native country, making the row architecturally fascinating. At number 2315 Massachusetts Avenue, the Embassy of Pakistan is an opulent 1908 mansion with a mansard roof and a rounded wall that hugs the corner. At 2349 is the 1905 Embassy of the Republic of Cameroon, one of the avenue's great early 20th-century Beaux Arts masterpieces. Opposite the Embassy of Ireland at 2234

stands a statue of the Irish revolutionary Robert Emmet (1778–1803), commissioned by Irish Americans to commemorate Irish independence. At 2536 is the India Supply Mission. Two carved elephants stand outside as symbols of Indian culture and mythology. The British Embassy at 3100 was designed by Edwin Lutyens in 1928. Outside is an arresting statue of Winston Churchill by William M. McVey.

Kalorama

E2 **M** **Woodley Park-Zoo/Adams Morgan, Dupont Circle**

A district of stately private homes and elegant apartment buildings, Kalorama (Greek for "beautiful view") has been home to the wealthy since its development at the turn of the 20th century as a suburb. Five presidents had homes here: Herbert Hoover, Franklin D. Roosevelt, Warren Harding, William Taft, and Woodrow Wilson. Some of the city's most striking and ornate

Mahatma Gandhi Memorial

E3 **2100-2120 Q St, NW, across the street from the Embassy of India** **M** **Dupont Circle**

In the park in front of the Indian Embassy stands a bronze statue of Mahatma

→
The striking Mahatma Gandhi Memorial statue

GREAT VIEW
Rock Creek Park

The best views of the stunning expanse of nearby Rock Creek Park (p171) are from Kalorama Circle at the northern end of 24th Street.

Gandhi by Indian sculptor Gautam Pal. Born Mohandas Karamchand Gandhi, the Mahatma became famous around the world for his ideas of ahimsa and non-violent protest against the colonial rule of Britain over India. In his later years he lived an ascetic's life, and the statue depicts him in simple garb during his 1930 Dandi March protesting against the British-imposed salt tax. Inscribed on the statue is Gandhi's philosophy: "My life is my message."

Lincoln Theatre

⑫ H2 **⑫** 1215 U St, NW **Ⓜ** U Street/African-Amer Civil War Memorial/Cardozo **⏲** 10am–6pm Mon–Fri **⏲** Federal hols **🌐** thelincolndc.com

Built in 1922, the Lincoln was once the centerpiece of cultural life for the city's African-American community. Like the landmark 1914 Apollo Theater in New York, the Lincoln presented big-name entertainment, such as pre-eminent jazz singers Ella Fitzgerald and Billie Holiday, and composer, pianist, jazz bandleader, and native Washingtonian Duke Ellington.

By the 1960s the area around the theater began to deteriorate, and by the 1970s the theater had closed down. Then, in the early 1980s, fundraising began for the $10-million renovation. Even the original, highly elaborate plasterwork was carefully cleaned and repaired, and the theater reopened in 1994.

Today, the Lincoln Theatre is a center for the performing arts, and is one of the cornerstones of the renaissance of U Street. The magnificent

→

The Woodrow Wilson House interior with its period furnishings

auditorium plays host to a year-around calendar of concerts, stage shows, and events, including Filmfest DC.

Woodrow Wilson House

⑬ D3 **⑬** 2340 S St, NW **Ⓜ** Dupont Circle **⏲** 10am–4pm Wed–Sat, noon–4pm Tue and Sun (summer: to 8pm Thu) **⏲** Federal hols **🌐** woodrowwilsonhouse.org

The former home of Woodrow Wilson (1856–1924), who was the president of the US from 1913 to 1921, is the only presidential museum within the District of Columbia.

Wilson led the US through World War I and advocated the formation of the League of Nations, the precursor to the United Nations. In 1919 Wilson collapsed from a stroke and became an invalid for the rest of his life. Many believe that Wilson's second wife, Edith Galt, assumed many of the presidential duties herself. Unable to leave his sickbed, Wilson saw his dream, the League of Nations, defeated in the Senate.

In 1920 Wilson was awarded the Nobel Peace Prize for his work on the League of Nations, and, at the end of his second term in 1921, he and his wife moved to this townhouse, designed by Waddy B. Wood. Edith Galt Wilson arranged for the home to be bequeathed to the nation. Since Wilson's death in 1924, the building has been maintained as it was during his lifetime, containing artifacts such as his Rolls-Royce and reflecting the style of an upper-middle-class home of the 1920s. The house today belongs to the National Trust for Historic Preservation.

BEYOND THE CENTER

A group of remarkable attractions lie scattered just beyond downtown. Arlington and Alexandria, settled in the early 17th century, were originally part of the British colony of Virginia, the site of vast plantations; they went on to become some of DC's first suburbs. To the south, Mount Vernon, George Washington's plantation, remains much as it was in his day. The National Cathedral to the north is arguably the city's most astounding and beautiful building, while the cheerful National Zoo nearby is perfect for kids. To the east is the National Arboretum, a 434-acre (175-ha) wonderland. In Anacostia, the Frederick Douglass National Historic Site is the home of the former slave who became a statesman and presidential advisor.

Must Sees

1. National Zoo
2. Mount Vernon
3. Washington National Cathedral
4. Old Town Alexandria

Experience More

5. The Pentagon
6. Arlington National Cemetery
7. Theodore Roosevelt Island
8. Iwo Jima Memorial (US Marine Corps War Memorial)
9. Hillwood Estate Museum and Gardens
10. Rock Creek Park
11. Kenilworth Park and Aquatic Gardens
12. National Arboretum
13. Frederick Douglass National Historic Site
14. Anacostia Community Museum
15. National Harbor

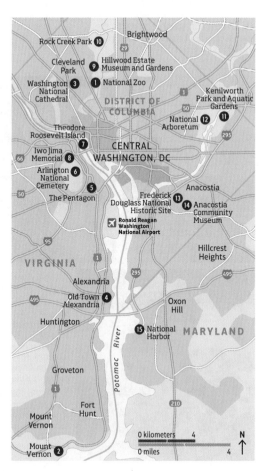

❶ ⊗ ▦ 🛍

NATIONAL ZOO

📍P3 🏛3001 Connecticut Ave, NW Ⓜ Cleveland Park, then 15-min walk, Woodley Park-Zoo/Adams Morgan 🕐Mid-Mar–Sep: 9am–6pm daily (buildings), 8am–7pm daily (grounds); Oct–mid-Mar: 9am–4pm daily (buildings), 8am–5pm daily (grounds) 🌐nationalzoo.si.edu

One of the city's most visited destinations, the National Zoo is not only a Noah's Ark of well-cared-for animals set in a beautifully land-scaped urban park but also an innovative center for conservation.

Established in 1889 as the Smithsonian's Department of Living Animals and sited on the Mall, the Smithsonian's National Zoo and Conservation Biology Institute moved to its present location in 1891. The park, which covers 163 acres (66 ha), was designed by Frederick Law Olmsted, the landscape architect responsible for New York's Central Park. Today, the zoo is home to more than 1,500 animals across 300 different species, many of which are endangered. The zoo also runs a number of breeding programs, the most successful of which are the cheetah and panda programs.

> 💬 INSIDER TIP
> **Snore & Roar**
>
> Drift off to the howls of the wolves and let the barks of the sea lions be your morning alarm. Have a wild time at the Snore & Roar Sleepovers with a fun nocturnal tour and an overnight campout in the zoo.

① The lush zoo welcomes about two million people annually.

② The "Great Cats" exhibit has two Sumatran tigers, the smallest of all tiger species, and a male Amur tiger, the largest of all cat species. Each can be recognized by their stripes - like human fingerprints, no two tigers have the same pattern.

③ The "Elephant Trails" exhibit provides an innovative, state-of-the-art home with diverse habitats to a small herd of Asian elephants, and is part of a campaign to save this endangered species.

↑ Visitors enjoying a playful
California sea lion at the
"American Trail" exhibit

 **2**

MOUNT VERNON

📍 P5 🏠 3200 Mount Vernon Memorial Hwy, VA (distillery on State Rte 235 S)
Ⓜ Huntington 🚌 Fairfax Connector 101 🕐 9am–5pm daily (Nov–Mar: to 4pm)
🌐 mountvernon.org

This graceful plantation house is the second most visited historic residence in America after the White House. No other place better portrays the character of the first US president, or the role of slavery-based agriculture in the young republic.

This country estate on the Potomac was George Washington's home for 45 years. The house was built as a farmhouse by his father, Augustine, but Washington made many changes, including adding the cupola and curving colonnades. The house is furnished as it would have been during Washington's presidency (1789–97), and visitors can explore its rooms, including the New Room, kitchen, Washington's study, and his bedroom, which contains the bed in which he died. The 500-acre (202-ha) grounds retain aspects of Washington's farm, with paddocks, stables, kitchen gardens, smokehouse, and slave quarters. The estate's wharf, once bustling with plantation shipping, still docks tour boats from the city – a lovely way to visit the estate. The orientation center and museum make fascinating bookends to a visit, with exhibits about Washington's life and career.

> 💬 INSIDER TIP
> **Watching History**
>
> Watch reenactments at the estate, including exciting restagings of wars and battles and a re-creation of George Washington's funeral. Check Mount Vernon's website for details.

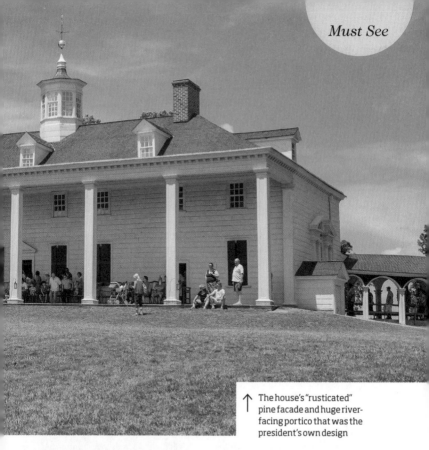

↑ The house's "rusticated" pine facade and huge river-facing portico that was the president's own design

1 With this unique 16-sided design, Washington invented one of the most aesthetic yet efficient treading barns. It allowed horses on the slatted upper floor to tread wheat stalks, with the separated grain falling through the slats into temporary storage below.

2 The impressive two-story New Room is formal yet inviting. Boards placed on trestles were used as a table as this was easier to clear for dancing.

3 Whiskey is still made and sold by the estate's reconstructed distillery.

3

WASHINGTON NATIONAL CATHEDRAL

N3 3101 Wisconsin & Massachusetts Aves, NW
Tenleytown/AU, Cleveland Park, then 25-min walk
32, 34, 36 10am–5pm Mon–Fri, 10am–4pm Sat, 8am–4pm Sun cathedral.org

The focus of the city's public spiritual life, the cathedral is the sixth largest in the world. Built on high ground, it dominates the city skyline and is DC's highest point.

The building of the Cathedral Church of Saint Peter and Saint Paul (its official name) began in 1907 and was completed in 1990. Built with Indiana limestone, the Washington National Cathedral boasts elements typical of Gothic religious architecture, including soaring vaulting, stained-glass windows, and intricate carvings. The exterior features fanciful gargoyles and dramatic sculpture. The cathedral has been the venue for funeral and memorial services for several US presidents.

INSIDER TIP
Specialty Tours

For ghouls, gargoyles, and grotesques, grab your binoculars and join the summertime tour exploring the whimsical carvings. Other tours include a tower climb, special photography access, a behind-the-scenes tour, in-depth tours on specialized topics, and a tea tour with scones and tea.

TOP 5 GARGOYLES AND OTHER GROTESQUES

Darth Vader (north)
Installed in 1986 on the cathedral's "dark" side.

Master Carver (north)
Salute to the cathedral's master carver Roger Morigi, holding a pistol, dagger, and flask in a tongue-in-cheek nod to Morigi's Italian heritage.

Yuppie (west)
A gargoyle grasping a briefcase, in honor of a New York executive.

Bishop (south)
A bishop wearing a stole and holding a crozier.

Evil Too (south)
A winged humanoid with its fingers in its ears, symbolizing evil refusing to listen to God.

The Washington National Cathedral, spiritual home of the nation

Pilgrim Observation Gallery

Ex Nihilo by Frederick Hart above the central portal, depicting people emerging from a swirling background

The west facade, dominated by three huge Gothic arches with pierced bronze gates

George Washington Bay

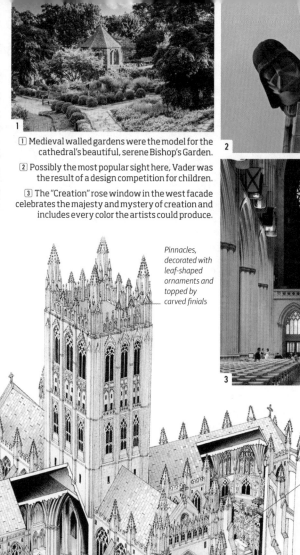

1 Medieval walled gardens were the model for the cathedral's beautiful, serene Bishop's Garden.

Must See

2 Possibly the most popular sight here, Vader was the result of a design competition for children.

3 The "Creation" rose window in the west facade celebrates the majesty and mystery of creation and includes every color the artists could produce.

Pinnacles, decorated with leaf-shaped ornaments and topped by carved finials

The high altar, with 110 figures surrounding the central statue of Christ

The Children's Chapel, built to the scale of a six-year-old, with statues of Jesus as a boy, and baby and mythical animals

The Space Window, with a piece of moon rock, marking mankind's scientific achievements

The nave, with iconography telling the story of humanity

The south rose window, depicting "The Church Triumphant"

Did You Know?

There are recitals at 12:30pm most Mondays and Wednesdays on the magnificent Aeolian-Skinner organ.

↑ Colonial houses lining the tree-shaded streets of Old Town Alexandria

4

OLD TOWN ALEXANDRIA

📍 P5 🏠 Alexandria, 8 miles (13 km) S of Capitol Hill
🚉 Alexandria Union Station Ⓜ King St-Old Town
ℹ 221 King St, www.visitalexandriava.com

Old Town Alexandria retains a Colonial flavor, dating back to its founding in 1749 as a port town. Still a busy seaport, it has tree-lined streets filled with historic sights. Restaurants are abundant here, art thrives, and the socializing goes on day and night in and around the pleasant Market Square.

① 🚲 Ⓜ 🛍

Carlyle House

🏠 121 N Fairfax St 🕐 10am–4pm Tue-Sat, noon–4pm Sun ⊘ Jan 1, Thanksgiving, Dec 25 🌐 novaparks.com/parks/carlyle-house-historic-park

An elegant Georgian Palladian mansion, this was built by wealthy Scottish merchant John Carlyle in 1753. It fell into disrepair in the 19th century but was bought in 1970 by the Northern Virginia Regional Park Authority and has since been beautifully restored. A tour provides fascinating details about 18th-century daily life. The garden has 18th-century plant species.

② 🚲 Ⓜ 🛍

Stabler-Leadbeater Apothecary Museum

🏠 105 S Fairfax St 🕐 Times vary, check website 🌐 alexandriava.gov/apothecary

Established in 1792, this family apothecary was in business for 141 years and is now a museum. Mahogany drawers still contain the potions noted on their labels, jars of herbal remedies line the shelves, and huge mortars and pestles and a collection of glass baby bottles are among its 8,000 original objects. George Washington was a patron, as was Robert E. Lee, who bought the paint for his Arlington house here.

③ 🚲 Ⓜ 🍴 🛍

Gadsby's Tavern Museum

🏠 134 N Royal St 🕐 Times vary, check website 🌐 alexandriava.gov/gadsbystavern

Dating from 1770, this pleasant tavern and the adjoining hotel, owned by John Gadsby, were the Waldorf-Astoria of their day. Now completely restored, they evoke the atmosphere of an old-time hostelry in this busy port. You can see the dining room with gaming tables, the bedrooms where travelers reserved not the room but a space in a bed, and the private dining room for the wealthy. The ballroom, where George and Martha Washington were fêted on his last birthday in 1799, can be rented out. This is also a working restaurant.

Did You Know?

A pew label in Christ Church reads "William E. Cazenove. Free pew for strangers."

④

Torpedo Factory Art Center

⌂ 105 N Union St ⏰ 10am-6pm daily (to 9pm Thu) 🚫 Jan 1, Easter, July 4, Thanksgiving, Dec 25 🌐 torpedofactory.org

Built as a torpedo factory during World War II, this was converted into an arts center by a partnership between the town and a group of local artists in 1974. Today there is gallery and studio space for over 80 artists to create and exhibit their work. Visitors can watch potters, sculptors, printmakers, and jewelry-makers at their craft.

⑤

Old Presbyterian Meeting House

⌂ 323 S Fairfax St ⏰ 8:15am-4:15pm Mon-Fri 🌐 opmh.org

Memorial services for George Washington were held in this 1772 meeting house. In the churchyard are buried Dr. John Craig, Washington's friend; the Reverend Muir, who officiated at Washington's funeral; and the American Revolution's unknown soldier.

⑥

Lee-Fendall House

⌂ 614 Oronoco St ⏰ 10am-4pm Wed-Sat, 1-4pm Sun 🌐 leefendallhouse.org

Philip Fendall built this stylish house in 1785, then married the sister of Revolutionary War hero "Light Horse" Harry Lee. Lee's descendants lived here until 1904. Artifacts from the Revolution to the 1930s Labor Movement fill the house.

⑦

Christ Church

⌂ 118 North Washington St ⏰ 9am-4pm Mon-Sat, 2-4:30pm Sun 🚫 Jan 1, Thanksgiving, Dec 25 🌐 historicchristchurch.org

The oldest continuously used church in town, this Georgian edifice was completed in 1773. George Washington's square pew still has his nameplate, as does Robert E. Lee's.

⑧

Farmers Market

⌂ Market Sq, King & Fairfax Sts ⏰ 7am-noon Sat

Dating back to 1753, just a few years after the city's founding in 1749, this pleasant market now sells fresh fruit and vegetables, herbs, meats, baked goods, cut flowers, and crafts. George Washington, a trustee of the market, regularly sent produce to be sold at the market from his farm at Mount Vernon *(p162)*.

NOTICE
ALL BOATS ARE PRIVATE
DO NOT BOARD
TRESPASSERS WILL BE PROSECUTED

Pier near the Torpedo Factory Art Center, Old Town Alexandria

EXPERIENCE MORE

The Pentagon

📍P4 🏛1000 Defense Pentagon, Hwy I-395, Arlington, VA Ⓜ Pentagon 🌐pentagontours.osd.mil

The Department of Defense, which includes the army, navy, and air force, is headquartered at the Pentagon. President Franklin D. Roosevelt decided in the early 1940s to combine the 17 buildings that comprised the department into one building. Construction of the Pentagon was started on September 11, 1941 and completed in January, 1943. Its five-sided design is very efficient, and despite its size, it takes only seven minutes to walk between any two points. On September 11, 2001, the building was damaged in a terrorist attack. A memorial to the 184 people who died here was dedicated on September 11, 2008. Tours are by appointment for US citizens only.

Arlington National Cemetery

📍B9 🏛Arlington, VA Ⓜ Arlington Cemetery 🕐Oct-Mar: 8am-5pm daily; Apr-Sep: 8am-7pm daily 🌐arlingtoncemetery.mil

Confederate General Robert Lee (1807–70) lived at Arlington House for 30 years. In 1861 he left to lead Virginia's armed forces, and the Union confiscated his estate for a military cemetery. Today, it is sobering to stroll through its 624 acres (252 ha), where a sea of white headstones mark 400,000

→

Rows of white marble headstones at Arlington National Cemetery

graves of soldiers, sailors, and airmen who gave their lives in conflicts from the Revolution to the present. The most popular stop is the Tomb of the Unknowns, which honors the unidentified soldiers who have died in battle. Visitors watch the changing of the guard at the tomb in silence. Another notable site is the grave of President Kennedy, who was assassinated in 1963. The eternal flame here was lit by his wife, Jackie, during his funeral and has burned since.

Theodore Roosevelt Island

📍C6 🏛GW Memorial Pkwy, McLean, VA Ⓜ Rosslyn 🕐6am-10pm daily 🌐nps.gov/this

A haven for naturalists, this island's 91 acres (37 ha) of marshland and forest are home to a variety of wildlife as well as many species of trees and plants. There are 2 miles (4 km) of nature trails, popular with bird-watchers. A bronze memorial statue honors President Theodore Roosevelt (1858–1919), who was an avid outdoorsman and naturalist.

GREAT VIEW
From the Iwo Jima Memorial

One of the best views in DC takes in the Lincoln Memorial, Washington Monument, US Capitol, and the Mall. It is also one of the best places to watch the fireworks on the Fourth of July.

Iwo Jima Memorial (US Marine Corps War Memorial)

📍B7 🏛Meade St between Arlington National Cemetery & Arlington Blvd Ⓜ Rosslyn

The horrific battle of Iwo Jima that took place during World War II was captured by press photographer Joe Rosenthal. His Pulitzer Prize-winning picture of six US Marines raising the American flag on the tiny Pacific island was magnificently translated into bronze by sculptor Felix DeWeldon in 1954. The Iwo Jima Memorial is dedicated to all members of the Marine Corps who have died defending their country.

A pretty stone bridge crossing Rock Creek in Rock Creek Park ↑

 9

Hillwood Estate Museum and Gardens

📍P2 🏠4155 Linnean Ave, NW Ⓜ Van Ness-UDC 🕐10am-5pm Tue-Sun ⊘Jan, Federal hols 🌐hillwoodmuseum.org

The 25-acre (10-ha) Hillwood Estate was owned by business-woman Marjorie Merriweather Post and opened to the public in 1977. The museum contains the most comprehensive collection of 18th- and 19th-century Russian imperial art to be found outside of Russia, including Fabergé eggs and Russian Orthodox icons, plus some renowned pieces of 18th-century French decorative art. The gardens on the estate, surrounded by wood-lands in the heart of the city, have important collections of azaleas and orchids.

 10

Rock Creek Park

📍P2 Ⓜ Cleveland Park 🌐nps.gov/rocr

Named for the creek flowing through it, the park is a 1,800-acre (728-ha) stretch of land that bisects the city from the Maryland border to the Potomac. It has a feeling of the wilderness, and foxes and deer are found in abundance. There are hiking and horse trails, a riding stable, tennis courts, a golf course, and the **Rock Creek Park Nature Center**. In the summer, the Carter Barron Amphitheater has rock, pop, jazz, and clas-sical concerts. On Sundays, a portion of Beach Drive, one of the park's main roads, is closed to cars to give cyclists and skaters freedom of the road.

Built in 1829, **Peirce Mill** was an active gristmill, driven by the creek's tumbling waters. Today, it is a working restora-tion, offering demonstrations from April to October. A large, elegant stone barn next to the mill serves as an art gallery.

Rock Creek Park Nature Center

📍P2 🏠5200 Glover Rd, NW Ⓜ Friendship Heights 🚌E4 🕐9am-5pm Wed-Sun ⊘Federal hols

Peirce Mill

📍P2 🏠2401 Tilden St, NW Ⓜ Van Ness-UDC 🕐Times vary, check website 🌐nps.gov/places/peirce-mill.htm

EAT & DRINK

2Amys

Family-friendly landmark with wood-fired Neapolitan pizza and Italian wines.

📍N2 🏠3715 Macomb St, NW 🌐2amysdc.com.

$$$

Barley Mac

This chic industrial space serves American classics with a modern twist.

📍A6 🏠1600 Wilson Blvd, Arlington 🌐barleymacva.com

$$$

Coppi's Organic Italian

Family owned and operated place offering northern Italian cuisine and wood-fired pizza .

📍P3 🏠3321 Connecticut Ave, NW 🌐coppisorganic.com

$$$

The Walrus Oyster and Ale

Extensive seafood menu features ten or more oyster varieties daily.

📍P5 🏠152 Waterfront St, Oxon Hill 🌐walrus oysterandale.com

$$$

Nanny O'Brien's

Traditional Irish pub with Guinness on tap and good pub food.

📍P3 🏠3319 Connecticut Ave, NW 🌐nannyobriens.com

$$$

↑ A pretty pagoda in the Japanese Garden at the National Arboretum

⑪ Kenilworth Park and Aquatic Gardens

◘ Q3 ▣ 1550 Anacostia Ave, NE Ⓜ Deanwood ◔ 9am–5pm daily (Nov–Mar: 8am–4pm) Ⓧ Jan 1, Thanksgiving, Dec 25 ◴ nps.gov/keaq

This tranquil park has 12 acres (5 ha) of natural wetland areas and historic ponds filled with water lilies and other aquatic plants from around the world. It was purchased in 1880 by Walter Shaw and his daughter Helen Fowler, who created the 20 or so ponds that are the centerpiece of Kenilworth and planted them with the water lilies and lotuses that the park is now known for. In late summer, the ponds are covered with pink blossoms. Wildlife includes otters, turtles, frogs, salamanders, and water birds. There are daily history and nature tours, and in the fall, weekend bird-watching tours.

⑫ National Arboretum

◘ Q3 ▣ 3501 New York Ave or 24th & R Sts off Bladensburg Rd, NE Ⓜ Stadium-Armory, then bus B2 ◔ 8am–5pm daily ◴ usna.usda.gov

Tucked away in a corner of northeast Washington is the hidden gem of the National Arboretum – a center for research, education, and the preservation of trees, shrubs, flowers, and other plants. This is a great place for families, offering a tram tour, grassy expanses where you can have a picnic, and lovely gardens and plantings. If you are lucky enough to be here in late April, the Azalea Collections boast thousands of brilliantly colored blooms bursting across the forest floor and along the winding footpaths of a wooded hillside.

The Japanese Garden includes the National Bonsai and Penjing Museum, with bonsai up to 380 years old. The herb garden has ten specialty gardens, grouping herbs according to use and historical significance. At the entrance to the garden is an elaborate 16th-century European-style "knot garden," with about 200 varieties of old roses. The National Grove of State Trees has trees representing every state.

⑬ Frederick Douglass National Historic Site

◘ Q4 ▣ 1411 W St, SE Ⓜ Anacostia ◔ 9am–5pm daily Ⓧ Jan 1, Thanksgiving, Dec 25 ◴ nps.gov/frdo

The African-American abolitionist leader Frederick Douglass lived in Washington toward the end of his illustrious career. After the Civil War he moved first to a townhouse on Capitol Hill, and then to Anacostia. In 1877 he bought this white-framed house, named it Cedar Hill, and lived here, with his family, until his death in 1895. During his time here, he made many improvements and, by the time of his death, Cedar Hill had grown to a 21-room mansion.

Douglass's widow opened Cedar Hill for public tours in 1903, and in 1962 the house was donated to the National Park Service. Most of the items on display are original and include gifts to Douglass from President Lincoln and the writer Harriet Beecher Stowe, author of *Uncle Tom's Cabin* (1852).

In the garden is a small stone building that Douglass used as an alternative study, and which he nicknamed "The Growlery." From the front steps of the house there is a magnificent view across the Anacostia River.

⑭ Anacostia Community Museum

◘ Q4 ▣ 1901 Fort Place, SE Ⓜ Anacostia ◔ 10am–5pm daily for tours ◴ anacostia.si.edu

Part of the Smithsonian, this museum examines the everyday issues that impact diverse

> ### FREDERICK DOUGLASS (1817-95)
> Born a slave around 1818, Frederick Douglass fought to end slavery in the United States. At the age of 20 he fled to Europe where British friends in the anti-slavery movement bought him from his masters, making him a free man. He lived mostly in New York, where he worked as a spokesman for the abolitionist movement. In 1847 he became editor of the anti-slavery newspaper *The North Star*. During the Civil War, Douglass advised President Lincoln and fought for constitutional amendments to guarantee equal rights to freed black people.

urban communities. The art, artifacts, photographs, documents, and sound recordings displayed here reflect the lives of the people living in the largely African-American and multiethnic neighborhoods east of the Anacostia River in Washington, DC. The museum hosts innovative exhibitions that are curated with the collaboration of members of the public.

With an extensive library and computers for visitors, the museum is as much a resource center as it is a space for art and history exhibitions.

INSIDER TIP
Oxon Hill Farm

Kids love this hands-on National Park farm, set just 3 miles (5 km) away from National Harbor, where they can pet farm animals and help with daily activities (www.nps.gov/oxhi).

15 🍴 🖥 🏛
National Harbor

📍P5 🏠165 Waterfront St, National Harbor, MD
Ⓜ King St-Old Town, Huntington, then bus
🌐nationalharbor.com

A glittering mini-city rising above the Potomac south of DC, National Harbor is a thriving center for shopping, dining, and entertainment. A waterfront walkway traces the edge of the river, inviting visitors to stroll past the marina and open plazas. The Capital Wheel is a favorite with older kids and a colorful carousel appeals to the little ones. In summer, there are free outdoor concerts and a giant screen that shows free movies. There are several ways to get out on the water, including kayak and canoe rentals, water taxis, and cruise boats. Nearby, the $1.3 billion MGM National Harbor luxury resort features a hotel, casino, and several restaurants.

STAY

Kimpton Glover Park Hotel
Serene luxury and attentive service, and coastal Italian cuisine in the on-site restaurant, Casolare.

📍N3 🏠2505 Wisconsin Ave, NW
🌐gloverparkhotel.com

$$$

AC Hotel by Marriott National Harbor
Sophisticated riverfront hotel at National Harbor, with chic rooms and suites, fitness center, and an outdoor terrace with river views.

📍P5 🏠156 Waterfront St, Oxon Hill, MD
🌐marriott.com

$$$

↑ The enormous Capital Wheel dominating the National Harbor waterfront walkway

DAYS OUT FROM WASHINGTON, DC

Within a short day's drive of Washington, DC lies enough history and natural beauty to satisfy the most insatiable sightseer. This area of Virginia and Maryland, along with parts of West Virginia and Pennsylvania, has been at the center of 400 years of turbulent American history. Founded in 1623, Jamestown was the first permanent English settlement in America. Nearby Williamsburg became the capital of Virginia in the 18th century, and the first colony to declare independence from England. Today, Historic Jamestowne and Colonial Williamsburg are both major attractions, with Williamsburg boasting 500 restored buildings and scores of costumed reenactors who bring the Colonial period to life. Chesapeake Bay and Annapolis are must-sees for history buffs, and both offer a wealth of dining and shopping opportunities. Lovers of the outdoors will find lots to do in Great Falls Park and on the islands of Chincoteague and Assateague. A drive west leads to the 105-mile (170-km) Skyline Drive, which offers stunning Blue Ridge Mountain scenery.

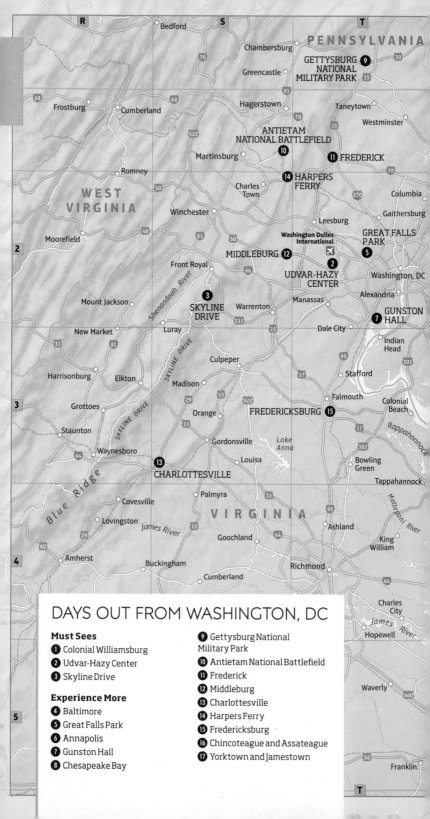

DAYS OUT FROM WASHINGTON, DC

Must Sees

1. Colonial Williamsburg
2. Udvar-Hazy Center
3. Skyline Drive

Experience More

4. Baltimore
5. Great Falls Park
6. Annapolis
7. Gunston Hall
8. Chesapeake Bay
9. Gettysburg National Military Park
10. Antietam National Battlefield
11. Frederick
12. Middleburg
13. Charlottesville
14. Harpers Ferry
15. Fredericksburg
16. Chincoteague and Assateague
17. Yorktown and Jamestown

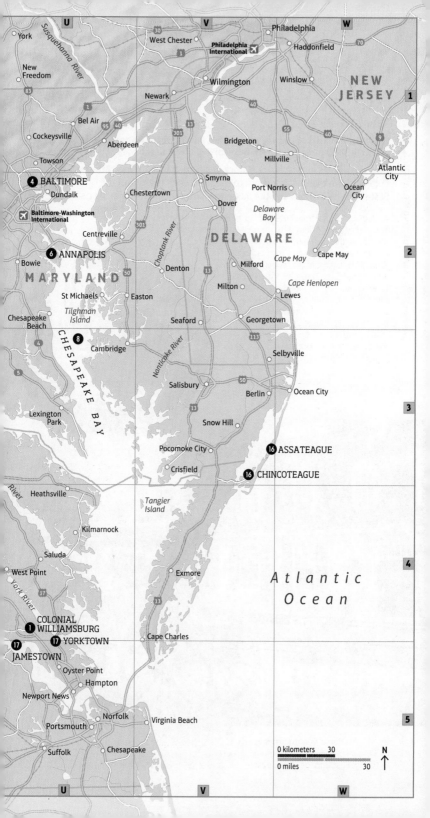

① ⌖ ✦ 🍴 🖥 🖶 🛍

COLONIAL WILLIAMSBURG

📍 U4 🚗 155 miles (250 km) S of Washington, DC 🚉🚌 ℹ 101 Visitor Center Dr; 9:15am–5pm daily; www.colonialwilliamsburg.com

Now the world's largest living history museum, this charming 18th-century Colonial town takes visitors back to the time when the idea of the United States was being born and the nascent country's ideals were being defined.

As Virginia's capital from 1699 to 1780, Williamsburg was the hub of the British colony. After the government moved to Richmond, the town went into decline. In 1926, John D. Rockefeller embarked on a restoration project. Today, in the midst of the modern city of Williamsburg, the 18th-century town has been re-created. Costumed interpreters reenact the lives of the original townspeople, craftsmen show off their skills, horse-drawn carriages clatter through the streets, and fife and drum bands play, vividly evoking America's past.

→

The reconstructed Governor's Palace, originally built in 1720

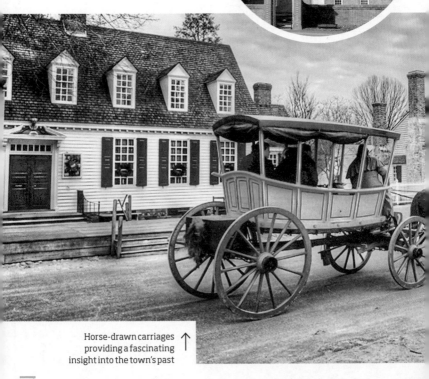

Horse-drawn carriages providing a fascinating insight into the town's past ↑

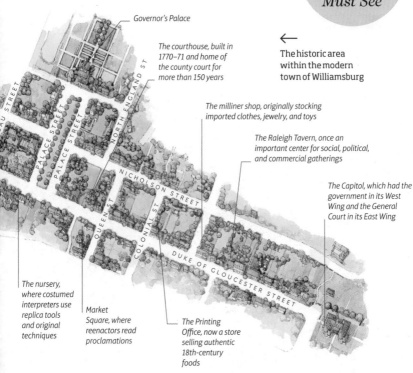

Governor's Palace

The courthouse, built in 1770–71 and home of the county court for more than 150 years

← The historic area within the modern town of Williamsburg

The milliner shop, originally stocking imported clothes, jewelry, and toys

The Raleigh Tavern, once an important center for social, political, and commercial gatherings

The Capitol, which had the government in its West Wing and the General Court in its East Wing

The nursery, where costumed interpreters use replica tools and original techniques

Market Square, where reenactors read proclamations

The Printing Office, now a store selling authentic 18th-century foods

Streets labeled: AU STREET, PALACE STREET, PALACE STREET, NORTH ENGLAND ST, NICHOLSON STREET, QUEEN ST, COLONIAL ST, DUKE OF GLOUCESTER STREET

Did You Know?

Buildings with a Grand Union flag in front are open to the public; all others are private.

The dazzling Boeing Aviation Hangar, enough to satisfy even the most avid flight fan ↑

2 ⓂⓄⓄⒶ

UDVAR-HAZY CENTER

📍 T2 🏠 14390 Air and Space Museum Pkwy, Chantilly, VA
Ⓜ Wiehle-Reston East, then Fairfax Connector 938
🕐 10am–5:30pm daily 🌐 airandspace.si.edu

The remarkable Steven F. Udvar-Hazy Center is a must for all enthusiasts of flight and space exploration. The museum is huge: just one of its two display hangars is the length of three football fields, ten stories high, and contains over 100 planes.

A companion to the National Air and Space Museum on the Mall in Washington *(p70)*, the center is home to the Space Shuttle *Discovery*, a Concorde supersonic jet, the B-29 Superfortress bomber *Enola Gay*, an SR-71 Blackbird spyplane, and thousands of other aviation and space artifacts. Visitors can climb up into an observation tower with a 360-degree view of nearby Dulles Airport to watch planes take off and land. Alongside the Boeing Aviation Hangar and the James S. McDonnell Space Hangar, also noteworthy is the Mary Baker Engen Restoration Hangar, where the preservation of the collection takes place. Visitors can watch restoration projects in progress from a glass-walled deck overlooking the hangar floor. Care has been taken to have plenty of kid-friendly activities, from an IMAX Theater to a squadron of flight simulators that offer experiences from a dogfight in a World War I triplane to flying a spaceship into a black hole. A Wall of Honor is a permanent testament to the men and women who have contributed to the heritage of aviation and space exploration.

TOP 5 LESSER-KNOWN AIRCRAFT AT UDVAR-HAZY

Boeing 307 Stratoliner
The first passenger airliner with a pressurized fuselage.

Pitts Special S-1C
Named *Little Stinker*, one of the most famous aerobatic planes.

Goodyear Pilgrim Gondola
Built in 1925 and part of Goodyear's first helium-filled airship.

Rutan Voyager
The first plane to fly nonstop around the world without a refueling stop.

Piper J-3 Cub
The most famous training craft, with thousands of pilots learning to fly in it.

① The observation tower at the Udvar-Hazy Center is open to visitors.

② The *Enola Gay*, a Boeing B-29 Superfortress, was the most advanced long-range bomber in World War II, and was the plane that dropped the first atomic bomb on Hiroshima, Japan.

③ The Lockheed SR-71 Blackbird, a long-range, high-altitude stealth spy plane, is the fastest jet-powered plane in the world.

The winding beauty of Skyline Drive, one of America's most scenic routes ↑

3

SKYLINE DRIVE

📍S2 🏛North entrance at Front Royal, central at Thornton Gap and Swift Run Gap, south at Rockfish Gap 🕐All year 🚫In inclement weather 🌐visitskylinedrive.org

One of the most beautiful and pastoral scenic drives on America's east coast, the 105-mile (170-km) Skyline Drive runs along the backbone of the Shenandoah National Park's Blue Ridge Mountains.

The road traces languidly serpentine curves high above the lush green Shenandoah River Valley, leading to 75 viewpoints that offer stunning natural scenery, as well as numerous hiking trails and points of interest. A good place to start is the Dickey Ridge visitor center from where you can get maps and guides and enjoy a splendid panoramic view of the valley. Park rangers lead a variety of hikes and programs, including a tour to the rustic camp that was President Herbert Hoover's private retreat until 1933, when he donated it to the park. Big Meadows is another popular stopping spot, with numerous hiking trails, three waterfalls, a restaurant, lodge, and campground. The large meadow for which the site was named provides a riot of color, with bright foliage in the fall and carpets of wildflowers in spring. Deer, wild turkey, black bears, bobcats, coyotes, and flying squirrels inhabit the park, and wildflowers, azaleas, and mountain laurel are abundant.

> **INSIDER TIP**
> **Signposting**
>
> There is no signage along the drive, so a knowledgable local guide can help you choose the exits that will take you to other attractions and restaurants that are located just a short distance outside Shenandoah National Park.

Did You Know?

Shenandoah has over 500 miles (804 km) of hiking trails of all difficulty levels.

[1] Stony Man Peak is a pleasant 1.5-mile (2.5-km) hike to rock ledges with spectacular views.

[2] An iconic 0.75-mile (1.2-km) trail leads down to the lovely Dark Hollow Falls.

[3] Wildlife sightings, including black bear, deer, and turkey, are common; rarer sightings include bobcat and coyote.

EXPERIENCE MORE

Baltimore

Q U2 **A** Chesapeake Bay, MD **🚗🚌** **ℹ** Inner Harbor West Wall; www.baltimore.org

There is much to do and see in this pleasant city. Start at the Inner Harbor, with its waterside complex of shops and restaurants. Its focus is the **National Aquarium**, with many fascinating exhibits. The harbor is also home to the **Maryland Science Center**, where "do touch" is the rule, and the planetarium and an IMAX® theater thrill visitors. Nearby, the **American Visionary Art Museum** has works by self-taught artists whose materials range from matchsticks to faux pearls.

Known for its ancient Egyptian art, the **Walters Art Museum**, a few blocks north, also includes pieces by Monet and Fabergé. Uptown is the **Baltimore Museum of Art**, with its peerless collection of modern art, including works by Matisse, Picasso, Degas, Van Gogh, and Warhol, and two sculpture gardens featuring work by Rodin and Calder.

The Little Italy area is worth a visit for its knockout Italian eateries and games of bocce (boules) played around Pratt or Stiles streets on warm nights.

National Aquarium
♿🛍 **A** 501 E Pratt St, Pier 3 **W** aqua.org

Maryland Science Center
♿🛍 **A** 601 Light St **W** mdsci.org

American Visionary Art Museum
♿🍴🛍 **A** 800 Key Hwy at Inner Harbor **W** avam.org

Walters Art Museum
♿🛍 **A** 600 N Charles St **W** thewalters.org

Baltimore Museum of Art
♿🍴🛍 **A** 10 Art Museum Drive **W** artbma.org

Great Falls Park

Q T2 **A** Georgetown Pike, Great Falls, VA **O** 7am–dusk daily **W** nps.gov/grfa

The first view of the falls, near the visitor center, is quite

Did You Know?

The Potomac narrows from 1,000 ft (305 m) above Great Falls to 60 ft (18 m) below, greatly increasing its force.

breathtaking. The waters of the Potomac roar through the jagged, rocky Mather Gorge over a 76-ft (23-m) drop. Only experienced kayakers are permitted to paddle the turbulent whitewater below, which varies in power with rainfall upstream. The park boasts 15 miles (24 km) of hiking trails, some showing evidence of the commerce from the early-19th-century Patowmack, America's first canal.

Annapolis

Q U2 **A** Anne Arundel County, MD **ℹ** 26 West St; www.visit-annapolis.org

Maryland's capital Annapolis is the jewel of Chesapeake Bay, defined by the distinct nautical

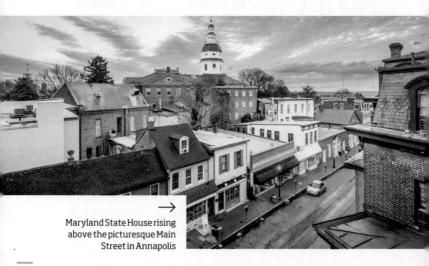

→ Maryland State House rising above the picturesque Main Street in Annapolis

→

Chesapeake Bay's Thomas Point Shoal Light, and exhibits at the Chesapeake Bay Maritime Museum *(inset)*

character that comes with 17 miles (27 km) of shoreline and the longtime presence of the US Naval Academy.

Main Street goes past the 200-year-old Maryland Inn to the City Dock. From here it is a short walk to the 150-year-old **US Naval Academy**, whose visitor center contains the Freedom 7 capsule that carried the first American, Alan Shepard, into space.

Annapolis teems with Colonial buildings, most of them still in everyday use. The **Maryland State House** is the oldest state capitol in continuous use. Delegates from the American colonies met here when Annapolis was briefly the nation's capital in 1783–4. **William Paca House**, home of Governor Paca, one of those who signed the Declaration of Independence, is a fine Georgian house with a pretty garden, both of which have been lovingly restored. The **Hammond Harwood House**, a Georgian masterpiece, has also been restored. The Duke of Gloucester and Cornhill streets are fine examples of the city's historic residential streets. Many tours are on offer in Annapolis, including by foot, bus, and boat.

US Naval Academy
⊛ 🄰 52 King George St
🅦 usna.edu

Maryland State House
⊛ 🄰 State Circle 🅦 msa.maryland.gov

William Paca House
⊛ 🄰 186 Prince George St
🅦 annapolis.org

Hammond Harwood House
⊛ 🄰 19 Maryland Ave at King George St 🅦 hammond harwoodhouse.org

7 ⊛ Ⓜ 🄰

Gunston Hall

🄰 T2 🄰 10709 Gunston Road, Mason Neck, VA
🄰 9:30am–6pm daily
🄰 Jan 1, Thanksgiving, Dec 25 🅦 gunstonhall.org

This Georgian house, built in 1755, was the home of George Mason, author of the 1776 Virginia Declaration of Rights. Situated 20 miles (32 km) south of Washington, DC, it is an exquisite example of careful historic restoration.

Of particular interest is the finely carved woodwork in the entrance hall, the Chinese-style mantel and woodwork over the fireplace in the formal dining room, and the servants' staircase that was used by the slaves so they wouldn't be seen by guests. Outside, the paths and gardens are lined with boxwood hedges that are more than 250 years old.

---

8 🍴 Ⓟ 🄰

Chesapeake Bay

🄰 U3 🅦 baydreaming.com

Called "the land of pleasant living," Chesapeake Bay offers visitors historic towns, fishing villages, pleasant bed-and-breakfasts, seafood restaurants, beaches, wildlife, and farmland. The **Chesapeake Bay Maritime Museum**, located in the small town of St. Michaels, depicts life

on the bay, both past and present. **Tilghman Island**, in the middle of Chesapeake Bay, has the last commercial sailing fleet in North America and hosts a popular seafood festival every June.

Chesapeake Bay Maritime Museum
🅦 cbmm.org

Tilghman Island
🅦 tilghmanisland.com

THE GETTYSBURG ADDRESS

The main speaker at the dedication of the National Cemetery in Gettysburg on November 19, 1863 was the orator Edward Everett. President Lincoln had been asked to follow with "a few appropriate remarks." His two-minute, 272-word speech paid tribute to the fallen soldiers, restated his goals for the Civil War, and rephrased the meaning of democracy: "government of the people, by the people, for the people." Inaudible to many, Lincoln declared the speech a failure. However, once published, it revitalized the North's resolve to preserve the Union, and today it is known to every schoolchild in America.

Gettysburg National Military Park

Q T1 **A** Gettysburg, PA **C** 6am-7pm daily (to 10pm Apr-Oct) **C** Jan 1, Thanksgiving, Dec 25 **W** nps.gov/gett

This 10-sq-mile (25-sq-km) park, south of the town of Gettysburg, Pennsylvania, marks the site of the three-day Civil War battle on July 1–3, 1863. It remains the bloodiest event ever to take place on American soil, with 51,000 casualties. Union victory ended Confederacy hopes for independence. A two- or three-hour driving tour begins at the **visitor center**. Free ranger-led walks interpret and explain the battle. On weekends (April–October) there are Living History reenactments. Other sights include the National Cemetery opposite, where Lincoln gave his Gettysburg Address, the David Wills House where he finalized the speech, and the Eternal Light Peace Memorial.

Visitor Center

A 1195 Baltimore Pike **C** 8am-5pm daily (to 6pm Apr-Oct)

Antietam National Battlefield

Q S1 **A** Rte 65, 10 miles (16 km) S of Hagerstown, Washington County, MD **C** Dawn-dusk daily (visitor center: 9am-5pm daily) **C** Jan 1, Thanksgiving, Dec 25 **W** nps.gov/anti

One of the worst battles of the Civil War was waged here on September 17, 1862. There were 23,000 dead, wounded, or missing, but no decisive victory. An observation tower offers sweeping battlefield views. Antietam Creek flows peacefully under Burnside Bridge. General Lee's defeat

inspired Lincoln to issue the Emancipation Proclamation. The visitor center has an excellent movie re-creating the historic battle.

Frederick

Q T1 **A** Frederick County, MD **i** 151 S East St; www.visitfrederick.org

This charming town's historic downtown was beautifully restored, and is now home to hundreds of antique dealers. The **National Museum of Civil War Medicine** displays tools and equipment used in the war to illustrate the medical practices of the time. **Rose Hill Manor Park** offers children hands-on experiences of the daily life of the first governor of Maryland and his family. Francis Scott Key, author of "The Star-Spangled Banner," is buried here in Mount Olivet Cemetery.

National Museum of Civil War Medicine

W civilwarmed.org

Rose Hill Manor Park

W recreator.com/264

$\rightarrow$

Cannon in front of the New York State Monument, Antietam National Battlefield

↑ Shopping street in picturesque Middleburg

12 (icons)

Middleburg

S2 Rte 50, Loudoun County, VA **12** N Madison St; open 11am–3pm Mon–Fri, 11am–4pm Sat–Sun; www.visitmiddleburgva.com

The horse is king in this little piece of England nestled in the foothills of Virginia's Blue Ridge Mountains. The town's history began in 1728, with Joseph Chinn's fieldstone tavern on the Ashby's Gap Road, still operating as the Red Fox Inn. The exquisite

countryside has a number of thoroughbred horse farms; Foxcroft Road, north of town, winds past some. In town, the **National Sporting Library & Museum** specializes in fine art depicting equestrian and other outdoor sports.

Dozens of wineries thrive in the area. Along John Mosby Highway are the **Chrysalis Vineyards** and the **Cana Vineyards and Winery**. Both have tours and tastings. **Aldie Mill Historic Park** nearby has tours of the 200-year-old mill on summer weekends.

National Sporting Library & Museum
📍 102 The Plains Road
🌐 nationalsporting.org

Chrysalis Vineyards
📍 39025 John Mosby Hwy
🌐 chrysaliswine.com

Cana Vineyards and Winery
📍 38600 John Mosby Hwy
🌐 canavineyards.com

Aldie Mill Historic Park
📍 39401 John Mosby Hwy
🌐 novaparks.com

EAT

Bertha's
"Eat Bertha's Mussels" with a pint of bitter at this fun seafood joint. Live music many evenings.

📍 U2 🏠 734 S Broadway, Baltimore, MD
🌐 berthas.com

Firestone's Culinary Tavern
Trendy gastropub with an extensive American menu and over 80 beers. The seared scallops are excellent.

📍 T1 🏠 105 N Market St, Frederick, MD
🌐 firestones restaurant.com

$$$

Whiskey Jar
Traditional Southern comfort food with local, seasonal ingredients, plus a whiskey bar.

📍 S3 🏠 227 W Main St, Charlottesville, VA
🌐 thewhiskeyjar cville.com

$$$

Red Hot and Blue Barbecue
Memphis-style hickory ribs and pulled pork are served in this family-friendly place with blues memorabilia.

📍 U2 🏠 200 Old Mill Bottom Rd S, Annapolis, MD 🌐 redhotandblue.com/annapolis

---

Sin Fronteras
Authentic Mexican and Latin American cuisine served in a tiny, cheerful restaurant. Great margaritas.

📍 U2 🏠 2129 Forest Dr, Annapolis, MD
🌐 sinfronterascafe.com

$$$

Crab Claw
This popular waterfront restaurant serves fresh seasonal Chesapeake Bay seafood. Full service bar.

📍 U2 🏠 304 Burns St, St Michaels, MD
🌐 thecrabclaw.com

$$$

13

Charlottesville

Q S3 **A** Virginia **🚌🚍** **🛈** 610
E Main St; www.visit
charlottesville.org

Charlottesville was Thomas Jefferson's hometown. It is dominated by the University of Virginia, which he founded and designed, and by his home, **Monticello**.

Jefferson was a Renaissance man: author of the American Declaration of Independence, US president, farmer, architect, inventor, and vintner. It took him 40 years, starting in 1769, to complete Monticello, now one of the country's most celebrated houses. The mansion's entrance hall doubled as a private museum, and its library held around 6,700 books. Tours of the house are available all year round.

Vineyards and wineries surround Charlottesville. Michie Tavern, joined to the Virginia Wine Museum, has been restored to its 18th-century appearance, and serves a buffet of typical Southern food. Montpelier, on a 2,500-acre

(1,000-ha) site 25 miles (40 km) to the north, was the home of US president James Madison.

Monticello

 A 931 Thomas Jefferson Pkwy, Rte 53
🕐 Times vary, check website
🌐 monticello.org

14

Harpers Ferry

Q S2 **A** Jefferson County, WV **🕐** Park: dawn–dusk daily; museums and contact stations: 9am–5pm daily **🕐** Jan 1, Thanksgiving, Dec 25 **🌐** nps.gov/hafe

Nestled at the confluence of the Shenandoah and Potomac rivers in the Blue Ridge Mountains is Harpers Ferry. The town, part of which is now a National Historical Park, was named for Robert Harper, a Philadelphia builder who established a ferry across the Potomac here in 1761. There are stunning views from Maryland Heights to the foot of Shenandoah Street, near abolitionist John Brown's fort.

Did You Know?

Harpers Ferry changed hands 14 times between Union and Confederate forces during the Civil War.

Brown's ill-fated 1859 raid on the Federal arsenal became tinder in igniting the Civil War. The historic importance of the town led to it being designated a national park in 1944.

15

Fredericksburg

Q T3 **A** Virginia **🚌🚍**
🛈 706 Caroline St; times vary, check website; www.visitfred.com

The town's attractions are its historic downtown district, and four Civil War battlefields, including the Wilderness where Confederate troops gained a tactical victory. Downtown, the Hugh Mercer

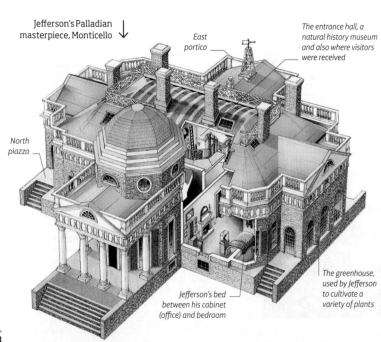

Jefferson's Palladian masterpiece, Monticello ↓

East portico

The entrance hall, a natural history museum and also where visitors were received

North piazza

Jefferson's bed between his cabinet (office) and bedroom

The greenhouse, used by Jefferson to cultivate a variety of plants

Apothecary Shop and Rising Sun Tavern offer living history accounts of life in a town that began as a Rappahannock River port. **Kenmore**, home of George Washington's sister Betty Washington Lewis, has some beautiful interiors.

Kenmore
 1201 Washington Ave
 kenmore.org

16

Chincoteague and Assateague

 V3 Accomack County, VA nps.gov/asis

These adjacent islands offer a wealth of natural beauty, and can be accessed by road from Virginia. Chincoteague is more developed, and has a town of the same name with the small **Museum of Chincoteague** displaying oyster-industry artifacts and model boats. A road from here offers access to Assateague Island, an unspoiled strip with a beach and hiking trails that wind through woods and marshes.

Assateague is famously populated by wild ponies, thought to be descended from animals grazed on the island by 17th-century farmers. Its woodlands and salt marshes attract over 300 species of birds, and in fall peregrine falcons and snow geese fly in. Monarch butterflies migrate here in October. There are several campgrounds in the area, and the ocean beach is ideal for swimming and surf fishing. The **Chincoteague National Wildlife Refuge** can provide more information on accommodation and activities.

Museum of Chincoteague
 7125 Maddox Blvd
 chincoteaguemuseum.com

Chincoteague National Wildlife Refuge
 8231 Beach Rd fws.gov/refuge/chincoteague

A replica of a colonists' ship, Historic Jamestowne ↑

17

Yorktown and Jamestown

 U5 York County & James City County, VA
 (757) 890-3300

Founded in 1607, Jamestown was America's first permanent English settlement. The site includes **Historic Jamestowne**, which features a museum and the ruins of the original settlement. There is a re-creation of James Fort, as well as full-scale reproductions of the first colonists' ships and a traditional Indian village.

Yorktown was the site of the decisive 1781 battle of the American Revolution. **Colonial National Historical Park**'s battlefield tours and exhibits explain the siege at Yorktown.

Historic Jamestowne
 1368 Colonial Pkwy, Jamestown historicjamestowne.org

Colonial National Historical Park
 1000 Colonial Pkwy, Yorktown nps.gov/colo

STAY

10 Clarke
Upscale Victorian B&B with a garden located in a tranquil historic area near downtown Frederick. Free three-course breakfast and evening cookies with wine.

 T1 10 Clarke Pl, Frederick, MD
 10clarke.com

$ $ $

Inn at Court Square
Luxury boutique inn set in two adjacent houses, beautifully furnished with antiques. Free parking and breakfast.

 S3 410 E Jefferson St, Charlottesville, VA
 innatcourtsquare.com

$ $ $

NEED TO KNOW

Washington, DC Metro station

BEFORE
YOU GO

Forward planning is essential to any successful trip. Be prepared for all eventualities by considering the following points before you travel.

AT A GLANCE

CURRENCY
US Dollar (USD)

AVERAGE DAILY SPEND

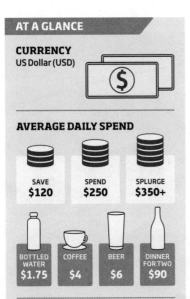

SAVE	SPEND	SPLURGE
$120	**$250**	**$350+**

BOTTLED WATER	COFFEE	BEER	DINNER FOR TWO
$1.75	**$4**	**$6**	**$90**

CLIMATE

 There are about 15 days of sun per month in winter, but nearly 20 days in summer.

 Temperatures range from an average of 1°C (34°F) in January to 26°C (79°F) in July.

 There is an average of 4 in (101 mm) of rain May through September, and it reaches its lowest ebb in late winter.

ELECTRICITY SUPPLY

The standard US electric current is 110 volts and 60 Hz. Power sockets are type A and B, fitting plugs with two flat pins.

Passports and Visas

Canadians and Mexicans need valid passports to enter the US. Citizens of Australia, New Zealand, and the EU do not need a visa, but must apply in advance for the Electronic System for Travel Authorization (**ESTA**) permit and have a valid passport. All other visitors need a passport and tourist visa, and will be photographed and have their fingerprints taken. A return ticket is required to enter the US. Entry regulations may change, so check in advance of travel with the US Department of State *(below)* for the most up-to-date visa and travel information.
ESTA
w esta.cbp.dhs.gov/esta

Travel Safety Advice

Visitors can get up-to-date travel safety information from the **US Department of State**, the **UK Foreign and Commonwealth Office**, and the **Australian Department of Foreign Affairs and Trade**.
Australia
w smartraveller.gov.au
UK
w gov.uk/foreign-travel-advice
US
w travel.state.gov

Customs Information

Passengers may carry the following into the US without incurring tax:
Tobacco products A carton of cigarettes, 50 cigars (not Cuban) or 2 kilograms (4.4 lbs) of smoking tobacco.
Alcohol A liter of alcohol as beer, wine, or liquor (if aged 21 years or older).
Cash If you are carrying $10,000 or more in cash (or other monetary instruments) you must declare it to the customs authorities.
Nonresident travelers need to complete a **Customs and Border Protection Agency** form when crossing the US border.
Customs and Border Protection Agency
w cbp.gov/travel

Insurance

Getting emergency medical insurance is highly recommended for international travelers to the US, as costs for medical and dental care can be very high. Travel insurance against trip cancellation, air travel delays, theft, and loss of belongings is also advisable. Car rental agencies offer vehicle and liability insurance, but check your policy before traveling.

Vaccinations

No inoculations are required for visiting the United States.

Money

Most establishments accept major credit, debit, and prepaid currency cards. Contactless payments are becoming increasingly common, but cash is usually required by smaller shops and businesses, street vendors, and on buses. Mobile payments on Washington, DC's Metro services are being rolled out in 2019.

Booking Accommodation

The city offers a wide range of accommodation options including high-rise hotels, historic inns, all-suites accommodations, budget B&Bs, and trendy boutique hotels.

Prices are lowest from January to March. Spring and summer are popular and generally expensive, although weekend rates may be lower when Congress is not in session. Book well in advance to secure the best deals. Rates are subject to an additional 14.5 percent room tax.

A comprehensive list of accommodation to suit all needs can be found on Destination DC, the city's official tourism website (p199).

Travelers with Specific Needs

Washington, DC is one of the most accessible cities in the US, but there are challenges involved with some historic buildings, restaurants, and shops.

MetroRail stations and trains are accessible, featuring extrawide fare-gates and elevators. Rail cars have gap reducers, priority seating, and emergency intercoms that also include instructions in Braille and raised alphabet. All MetroBuses are wheelchair friendly and have lifts or ramps for easy access. Visitors can find more information about public transport accessibility on the **Metro** website.

Government buildings, museums and theaters are generally accessible, but it is always best to call ahead to ensure that any specific requirements will be met.

Destination DC (p199) provides detailed information, tips, and general assistance for visitors with specific needs.

Metro
w wmata.com/accessibility

Language

Washington, DC is a cosmopolitan city in which you will hear multiple languages spoken. Many attractions and tour companies cater for those with limited English by offering foreign language headsets, museum guides and information packs. Some offer guided tours in different languages.

Closures

Monday Many museums close on Mondays.
Sunday Most banks close at 3pm and smaller businesses close for the day.
Federal and State Holidays Museums, public attractions, and many businesses close, especially for major holidays such as Thanksgiving and Christmas. Check with individual venues for specific opening and closing times.

FEDERAL HOLIDAYS 2020	
1 Jan	New Year's Day
20 Jan	Martin Luther King, Jr. Day
17 Feb	President's Day
25 May	Memorial Day
4 Jul	Independence Day
7 Sept	Labor Day
26 Nov	Thanksgiving Day
25 Dec	Christmas Day

GETTING
AROUND

Whether exploring Washington, DC's historic sights by foot or public transport, here is all you'll need to know to navigate the city like a pro.

AT A GLANCE

PUBLIC TRANSPORT COSTS

$2
MetroBus one-way

$2
MetroRail one-way (off-peak)

$14.75
MetroRail day pass

SPEED LIMIT

INTERSTATE HIGHWAY
55 mph (88 km/h)

MAIN ROADS
25 mph (40 km/h)

URBAN AREAS
25 mph (40 km/h)

SCHOOL ZONE
15 mph (24 km/h)

Arriving by Air

Three major airports serve Washington, DC. International flights arrive at Dulles International Airport, internal flights arrive at Reagan National Airport (DCA), and Baltimore-Washington International Airport (BWI) is a hub for low-cost international and internal flights.

Wiehle-Reston East is the nearest Metro station to Dulles, from which there is the connecting Washington Flyer Silver Line Express Bus to the airport. Travel time from the city center is over an hour. A quicker option is the Super-Shuttle share-ride bus service; it runs every hour, and pick-ups must be arranged in advance.

Reagan is served by the blue and yellow Metro lines. Travel time to and from downtown Washington is around 20 minutes.

Amtrak trains run every hour from 4am to 10pm from Union Station to Baltimore–Washington International, but a cheaper option is the MARC service from Union Station every hour from 6am to 10:30pm (weekdays only). For more information on journey times and pricing between the airport and downtown, see the table opposite.

Domestic Train Travel

Amtrak is one of the best ways to travel to the DC area. Trains from other cities arrive in Washington at Union Station. Trains are also available from Union Station to Baltimore, Philadelphia, Richmond, and Williamsburg. Amtrak offers a deluxe train service to New York City, called the Acela, which is slightly faster and more comfortable than the regular train, but is more expensive. Amtrak has a reduced-fare USA Rail Pass, which is worth considering if traveling widely across the country.

Trains (Acela or the slower Northeast Regional) to New York leave every hour. **MARC**, Maryland's commuter train, departs on weekdays for Baltimore.

Amtrak
w amtrak.com
MARC
w mta.maryland.gov

GETTING TO AND FROM THE AIRPORT

Airport	Transport	Price	Journey Time
Dulles International	Washington Flyer Silver Line Express	$6.75	1 hr 30 mins
	SuperShuttle	from $35	from 30 mins
	Taxi	$65	30 mins
Reagan National	MetroRail	from $6	20 mins
	SuperShuttle	from $15	from 20 mins
	Taxi	$25	20 mins
Baltimore-Washington International	Maryland Rail Commuter Service (MARC)	from $7	35 mins
	Amtrak	from $15	20 mins
	SuperShuttle	$37	from 1 hr
	Taxi	$30	1 hr

Public Transportation

Washington Metropolitan Area Transit Authority (**WMATA**) is Washington, DC's main public transportation provider. Find timetables, ticket information, maps, and more on the WMATA website.
WMATA
w wmata.com

Tickets
Tickets for the Metro and rechargeable SmarTrip cards can only be purchased at Metro stations, and bus tickets can only be bought on a bus.

MetroRail
For most destinations in the city, MetroRail, the subway-surface rail system, is the best way to get around.

The Metro consists of six color-coded lines: Red, Blue, Orange, Yellow, Green, and Silver. Trains run from 5am to 11:30pm Monday through Thursday, from 5am to 1am on Friday, from 7am to 1am on Saturday, and from 8am to 11pm on Sunday. Trains run frequently (every 10 minutes or less) and stops are announced at every station. Peak times (5–9:30am and 3–7pm Monday–Friday) are best avoided.

The cost of the fare depends on the time and distance you wish to travel, and the base fare starts from $2 off-peak and $2.25 at peak times. It is more expensive to travel during rush hour.

Tickets, or "farecards," for single or multiple trips can be bought from vending machines. Coins and bills (but no bills over $20) can be used to pay the exact fare; or add more money if you wish to use the card again. Customers will be able to pay for travel with their smartphones by 2019.

Passengers need to swipe their farecards through the turnstile at the beginning and end of the trip.

MetroRail passes are available for one day ($14.75) and seven days ($38.50). These can be used to transfer from MetroRail to MetroBus. SmarTrip cards are also available. These plastic rechargeable farecards cost $2 and can be used on other modes of public transportation in DC, and other regional transit systems.

Each Metro station works on three levels: street level, where you enter; mezzanine, where ticket machines are located; and the platform, which is accessed by escalator or elevator. Use the Metro map to work out which line you need for your destination and the terminus you will be heading for. The terminus denotes the direction the train is traveling and will be on signs in the station, guiding you to the correct platform. Where there is more than one line, follow the signs first for the line that you want and then the platform.

To get to the train, put your ticket in the access gate and retrieve it before passing through. If using a SmarTrip card, touch the circular disk on the gate once. Retain your ticket: it will be needed to exit the station.

Check the WMATA website for regular updates on travel disruptions and closures due to track maintenance.

MetroBus

MetroBus is a fast, inexpensive way to get around Washington, DC and connect to numerous outlying districts.

Fares can be paid either with exact change when you board the bus, with a SmarTrip card, or a MetroRail farecard pass which can be purchased online. Transfers are free within a three-hour period for SmarTrip card users. All other tickets are non-transferable; if changing buses you will need to pay for a new fare. Up to two children under the age of five can travel for free with a fare-paying passenger, and there are discounts available for disabled travelers and senior citizens.

Bus stops are identified by red, white, and blue signs. Signs list details of routes taken by all buses that use that stop. The bus will display both the route number and its terminus. Buses do not stop automatically; you will need to flag one down at a designated stop if you wish to board. Stops are announced on board. Pull on the line running along the top of the windows to request a stop. Always exit the bus at the back.

The **DC Circulator** bus is a popular choice for visitors. It links most of Washington, DC's main sights and attractions, and runs every 10 minutes. Fares are $1 for adults and 50 cents for children (under-5s travel free with a paying adult).

Maps of all the bus routes are available in MetroRail stations, and maps of specific lines are posted at each bus stop.

DC Circulator
🆆 dccirculator.com

Long-Distance Bus Travel

Intercity buses are an excellent, economical way to get to Washington, DC. As well as the traditional Greyhound buses, there are half a dozen bus companies serving DC, including **Megabus**, **Bolt Bus**, and the **Washington Deluxe**. Many of their buses are equipped with restrooms and free Wi-Fi.

Tickets are sold on a scale – a one-way ticket to New York generally costs about $30, but may end up costing as little as $1 with advance purchase, which is always cheaper than buying on the day.

Greyhound buses depart from the bus terminal near Union Station, but many of the other bus companies leave from more central locations throughout the city.

Bolt Bus
🆆 boltbus.com
Greyhound
🆆 www.greyhound.com
Megabus
🆆 megabus.com
Washington Deluxe
🆆 washny.com

Bus Tours

Several companies offer bus tours of DC's historic surroundings. **Gray Line** takes you on the Black Heritage tour, to Gettysburg National Military Park, Colonial Williamsburg, or Jefferson's home, Monticello. Several companies offer open-top tours. Passengers can hop on and off at any stop, and one- or two-day passes are available. **City Sights DC** organizes combination day trips covering Washington, DC's most popular landmarks, monuments and points of interest.

City Sights DC
🆆 citysightsdc.com
Gray Line
🆆 graylinedc.com

Taxis

There are designated taxi ranks across the city. In addition taxis wait near major sights, offices, and hotels, or can be hailed on the street. Taxis indicate that they are available by switching on the sign on the roof, and they will typically accept up to four passengers. All taxis are metered, and there are more than 100 companies from which travelers can choose.

The DC Taxi Cab Commission can provide names of reliable cab companies. Taxi fares in DC are operated using time and distance meters. Passengers should expect to pay a starting "drop" rate of $3.50, and then $2.16 for every mile after this. Luggage, extra pick-ups, and rush hour travel can all incur surcharges.

Taxis charge $25.00 per hour for waiting. Be aware that drivers do not always know the way to addresses beyond the tourist center.

Taxi app companies such as Uber also operate in the city.

DC Taxi Cab Commission
🆆 dfhv.dc.gov

Driving

There is much to see beyond Washington's city limits, and traveling by car is easy with a good map. However, driving is not the most efficient way to get around in the core DC area. There are one-way streets, time-of-day parking restrictions, and few gas stations. Avoid rush hour (5–9:30am and 3–7pm Monday–Saturday).

Washington, DC's road network forms a grid. Most numbered streets run north and south, and most lettered streets run east and west. Diagonal streets running at a 45-degree angle crisscross the grid in both directions and have a full road name, usually the name of a state.

Addresses contain NE, SE, SW, or NW, indicating their position relative to the Capitol building, which is at the center of the grid.

Every addresss in DC includes the quadrant code, and its use is necessary to distinguish the precise location you are trying to reach.

Be aware that there is no "J", "X", "Y" or "Z" Street, and "I" Street is written as "Eye" Street.

Car Rental

Rental car companies are located at airports, Union Station, and many other locations.
To rent a car in the US you must be at least 25 years old with a valid driving license and a clean record. All agencies require a major credit card.

Getting damage and liability insurance is recommended. It is advisable to return the car with a full tank of gas, otherwise you will be required to pay the inflated fuel prices charged by the rental agencies. Check for any pre-existing damage to the car and make sure you note this on your contract.

Parking

Parking in a lot will cost you about $25 per day or about $12 for two hours. Street parking meters have a two-hour maximum stay, and fines are high.

Parking is prohibited on many downtown streets during rush hour. You can find specific time restrictions signposted on curbside signs. Your car will be towed if you disregard them.

Gasoline (Petrol)

Gas comes in three grades – regular, super, and premium. There is an extra charge if an attendant serves you, but patrons can fill their own tanks at self-service pumps without incurring an extra fee. Most stations are exclusively self-service and only accept credit cards. Gas is generally cheap in the US.

Rules of the Road

All drivers are required to carry a valid driver's license and must be able to produce registration documents and insurance for their vehicle. Most foreign licenses are valid, but if your license is not in English, or does not have a photo ID, you must get an International Driving Permit (IDP) in advance of your trip.

Traffic drives on the right-hand side of the road. Seat belts are compulsory in front seats and suggested in the back; children under three must ride in a child seat in the back. Belts are also compulsory in cabs.

You can turn right at a red light as long as you first come to a complete stop, and if there are no signs that prohibit it. A flashing yellow light at an intersection means slow down, look for oncoming traffic, and proceed with caution. Passing (overtaking) is allowed on any multilane road, and you must pass on the left. On smaller roads safe passing places are shown by a broken yellow line on your side of the double-yellow line.

Crossing a double-yellow line, either by U-turn or by passing the car in front, is illegal, and will incur a fine if caught.

If a school bus stops to let passengers off, all traffic from both sides must stop and wait for the bus to drive off.

A limit of 0.08 percent blood alcohol is strictly enforced. For drivers under the age of 21 there is a zero tolerance policy for drink-driving. Driving while intoxicated (DWI) is a punishable offense that incurs heavy fines or even a prison sentence. Do not drink if you plan to drive.

In the event of an accident or breakdown, drivers of rental cars should contact their car rental company first. Members of the American Automobile Association (**AAA**) can have their vehicle towed to the nearest service station for repairs.

AAA
w aaa.com

Cycling

There is a handy network of cycle routes throughout the city, with some main roads offering dedicated cycle lanes.

Capital Bikeshare has bicycles for hire at around 300 locations. One-day, three-day, or monthly passes are available. **Bike and Roll** offers bike rentals, as well as organized tours of the city. Rentals can be made by phone or in-store from a minimum of 2 hours ($15) to a maximum of one day ($35). They provide helmets, some equipment such as locks, bicycle pumps, and puncture repair kits, as well as bicycle route maps of the city.

Some cycle lanes are also used by buses and taxis. Bicycles can be taken on buses, but must be stowed on racks at the front.

Bike and Roll
w bikeandrolldc.com
Capital Bikeshare
w capitalbikeshare.com

Walking

Washington is a city built for walking, with numerous green spaces, wide sidewalks, and courteous drivers. Busy streets have pedestrian walk lights at intersections.

While many of the main sights and monuments are clustered around the Mall, other attractions are quite spread out, so be sure to pack a pair of comfortable shoes.

Allow around two hours to cover the main sights from the Washington Monument to the Lincoln Memorial and around the Tidal Basin. If you get tired of walking, you can hop on the DC Circulator (*p196*) to see the sights from a city bus. Beware that traffic can be slow moving.

PRACTICAL
INFORMATION

A little local know-how goes a long way in Washington, DC. Here you will find all the essential advice and information you will need during your stay.

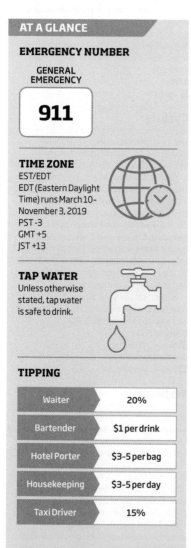

AT A GLANCE

EMERGENCY NUMBER

GENERAL EMERGENCY

911

TIME ZONE
EST/EDT
EDT (Eastern Daylight Time) runs March 10–November 3, 2019
PST -3
GMT +5
JST +13

TAP WATER
Unless otherwise stated, tap water is safe to drink.

TIPPING

Waiter	20%
Bartender	$1 per drink
Hotel Porter	$3-5 per bag
Housekeeping	$3-5 per day
Taxi Driver	15%

Personal Security

Washington is a large, cosmopolitan city and is generally safe in the tourist areas. Petty crime does exist, so be alert to your surroundings. Be wary of pickpockets on public transport and in crowded tourist areas.

If you have anything stolen, report the crime within 24 hours to the nearest police station and take ID with you. If you need to make an insurance claim, get a copy of the crime report.

Contact your embassy if you have your passport stolen, or in the event of a serious crime or accident.

Health

For ease of moving through airport security, pack any items of essential medication in their original labeled containers. Unused syringes are allowed through airport security along with any injectable prescription medication such as insulin.

It is possible to visit a doctor or dentist without being registered with them, but you will be asked to pay in advance. Keep all receipts for medical costs to make a claim on your insurance.

Pharmacists, such as CVS, are usually able to offer basic medical advice and prescriptions. Some pharmacies have clinics attached to treat common illnesses and minor injuries. One such clinic is the **CVS Minute Clinic**, which has six locations in DC. For immediate treatment in an emergency, call 911 for an ambulance.

Payment of hospital bills and other medical expenses is the patient's responsibility. As such it is important to arrange comprehensive medical insurance (p193) before traveling.
CVS Minute Clinic
w minuteclinic.com

Smoking, Alcohol, and Drugs

Smoking is prohibited in all enclosed public spaces. Cigarettes can be purchased by those over 18 years old; proof of age is required.

The legal minimum age for drinking alcohol in Washington is 21, and you will need photo ID

as proof of age. It is illegal to drink alcohol in public parks or to carry an open container of alcohol in your car, and penalties for driving under the influence of alcohol are severe *(p197)*.

Possession of illegal drugs is prohibited and could result in a prison sentence.

ID

It is not compulsory to carry ID at all times in Washington, DC. If you are asked by police to show your ID, a photocopy of your passport (and visa if applicable) should suffice.

Local Customs

Be respectful when visiting national monuments and sights of national significance.

You can be fined for littering. Dispose of your waste in garbage cans. Use the blue bins on the National Mall and in most museums to recycle bottles and cans.

Visiting Churches and Cathedrals

Dress respectfully: cover your torso and upper arms; ensure shorts and skirts cover your knees.

Mobile Phones and Wi-Fi

Free Wi-Fi is available in all underground MetroRail stations. Cafés and restaurants will usually permit the use of their Wi-Fi on the condition that you make a purchase.

Cell phone service in Washington is excellent. If you are coming from overseas and want to guarantee that your cell phone will work, make sure you have a quad-band phone. Check with your service provider before you travel; you may also need to activate the "roaming" facility.

Other options include buying a prepaid cell phone in the US or a SIM chip for a US carrier.

Mail

Stamps can be purchased from most major supermarkets and in post offices – most are open from 9am to 5pm Monday to Friday, with a limited Saturday service, usually 9am to noon.

Blue mailboxes are for letters only. Small packages must be taken to a post office.

Depending on how far the mail needs to travel in the US, it can take from one to five days to arrive at its destination.

Taxes and Refunds

Taxes will be added to hotel and restaurant charges, theater tickets, some grocery and store sales, and most other purchases. Always check if tax is included in the price displayed. Sales tax is 6 percent, hotel tax is 14.5 percent, and there is a 10 percent tax on food and beverages.

When tipping in a restaurant, it is the norm to include the tax in your calculation. A quick way to calculate restaurant tips is simply to double the tax, which adds up to about 18 percent.

Discount Cards

Washington, DC offers a number of visitor passes and discount cards (available online and from participating tourist offices) for exhibitions, events, museum entry and even transport, such as **The DC Explorer Pass** and **The Washington DC Sightseeing Pass**. These cards are not free, so consider carefully how many of the offers you are likely to take advantage of before purchasing one.

Entry to all Smithsonian institutions, including the Air and Space Museum and National Zoo, is free.

The DC Explorer Pass
w smartdestinations.com/washington-dc
The Washington DC Sightseeing Pass
w sightseeingpass.com/en/washington-dc

WEBSITES AND APPS

DC Eater
Check out dc.eater.com for the latest restaurant news and food events.
DC Metro and Bus
Real-time rail and bus predictions from WMATA at www.wmata.com.
Destination DC
Visit Washington, DC's official tourism website at washington.org.
Smithsonian Mobile
A digital guide to the Smithsonian featuring opening hours, floor plans and special events at www.si.edu/mobile.

INDEX

ACKNOWLEDGMENTS

Key: a-above; b-below/bottom; c-centre; f-far; l-left; r-right; t-top

Caption in 1795: Detail of mural by Allyn Cox 24tl; Ken Howard 10clb; Ian Dagnall Commercial Collection 126cl; imageBROKER 72-3t, 165cr; JeffG 13br, 146-7; LOOK Die Bildagentur der Fotografen GmbH 26-7b; MediaPunch Inc 111clb; Andrei Medvedev 130b; Mira 29crb; W. G. Murray 100tr, 127tl; National Geographic Creative 131t; Newscom 142-3t; NG Images 42bl; North Wind Picture Archives 109tl; NPS Photo 183bl; Michele Oenbrink 22bl; Efrain Padro 80-1b; Painting 92br; Sean Pavone 12tl, 85b, 98b, 115b, 144-5tl; Chuck Pefley 139bl; Pictorial Press Ltd 141tc; Herb Quick 12-3b; M Ramírez / Robert Berks Studio Inc- All rights reserved Albert Einstein Centennial Monument (1979) 36tr; Cheryl Rinzler 58bl, 124b, 137bl; RosalreneBetancourt 10 187tl; Philip Scalia 13t, 150bl; Kumar Sriskandan 96br; Mark Summerfield 22cr, 156tl, 185cra; Dennis Tarnay; Jr. 171tl; The Granger Collection 31cl; The Protected Art Archive 153bc; Gary Tognoni 27crb, 173b; Travelwide / Robert Berks Studio Inc. -All Rights Reserved John F. Kennedy bust (1971) 35br; Tribune Content Agency LLC 81tc; Steve Tulley / Monitor Korean War Veterans Memorial Foundation, Inc., Memorial Design - Korean War Veterans Memorial Advisory Board, Architects- Cooper and Lecky Architects; Inc., Sculptor - Frank Gaylord, Muralist - Louis Nelson 84t; Valentin Valkov 141ftr; Michael Ventura 96-7t, 123cr; Vespasian 144bc; WENN Ltd / © Niki de Saint Phalle Charitable Art Foundation / ADAGP, Paris and DACS, London 2018 One of Three Graces Statues (1999) 99tc; Tracey Whitefoot / © Neil Estern Franklin Delano Roosevelt and his dog, Fala Presidential Memorial (1997) 8cl; World History Archive 141tl; Jennifer Wright 55br, 70bl; ZUMA Press; Inc. 37cl.

Arena Stage at the Mead Center for American Theater: Nic Lehoux / Bing Thom Architects 18bl, 132-3.

Bridgeman Images: American Antiquarian Society, Worcester, Massachusetts / American School A Philosophic Cock (1804) 30-1b.

C&O Canal National Historical Park: Roy Roberts 122cr.

Depositphotos Inc: mannaggia 44t.

Dreamstime.com: Americanspirit 95tl, Mihai Andritoiu / © Felix De Weldon Iwo Jima Memorial (1995) 19tr, 158-9; Jon Bilous 8cla, 17br, 26-7t, 33crb, 87br, 104-5, 122-3b, 123tr, 165tl, 166t, 182-3t; Hunter Bliss 32t; Bratty1206 17tl, 88-9; Orhan Çam 61br; Chiyacat / Robert Indiana © Morgan Art Foundation Ltd. / Artists Rights Society (ARS), New York, DACS, London 2018 AMOR (2006) 41cl; Giuseppe Crimeni 139br; Cvandyke 27cla, 172tc; Dinhhang 42cl; F11photo 75cra, 75crb; Flashbacknyc 183crb; Richard Gunion 136-7t; SKmiragaya 74, 139cra; Erik Lattwein 160clb; Ltisha 143b; Nickjene 117c; OnAir2 109ftr; Sean Pavone 58-9tc, 184b; William Perry 112tc; ZHI QI 40-1b; Sborisov 108-9b; Daniel Thornberg 186-7b; Zrfphoto 28bl.

Dumbarton Oaks Research Library And Collections, Washington, D.C.: 125t.

Farmers Group Restaurants: Ken Flecther 42cla.

Getty Images: AFP / Eva Hambach 41tr; 165tr, /Jewel Samad 39cla, / Karen Bleier 75bl, 160crb, / Saul Loeb 43tr, 43bl, 111crb, / Paul J. Richards 37t, 43cl; Doug Armand 10-1bc; Bettmann 31tr, 45tl, 45tr, 46bl,101cr; Sisse Brimberg 2-3; Buyenlarge 157br; Matthew T. Carroll 48-9; The Christian Science Monitor / Andy Nelson 160bl; Call Group / Tom Williams 42cr; ClassicStock / Charles Phelps Cushing 44br; Corbis Historical 45bl; CQ-Roll Call Group / Bill Clark 13cr, / Tom Williams 42cr; DEA / Archivio J Lange 82bc; Grant Faint 42cla; Rick Friedman 47cra; Kenneth Garrett 123br; Jon Hicks 103tl; Hulton Archive 31br, 80tr, / Alex Wong 110br; Julie Thurston Photography 32-3b; David Hume Kennerly 25br; L. Toshio Kishiyama 178-9b; Lambert 25tr; The LIFE Picture Collection / Francis Miller 47tr; LOOK-foto / Elan Fleisher 138 Loop Images / John Greim 163clb; MikeBagley64 185tr; Mooney Photography / Kelly 18tl, 118-19; MPI 46cr; National Archives 46br; Richard T. Nowitz 82-3t; Marc Perrella 170-1b; Photolibrary / Barry Winiker 108cra; Caroline Purser 190-1b; Astrid Riecken 43br; George Rinhart 109tc; SuperStock 45bc; Universal History Archive 29cla, 46tl, 46-7tc; Visions Of Our Land 54bl; VisionsofAmerica / Joe Sohm 55fbr; The Washington Post 12bl, 22crb, 38br, 101b, 137cr, 152t, / Jahi Chikwendiu 43tl, / Katherine Frey 42cra, 161, / Marvin Joseph 42br, / Nikki Kahn 43cr, / Matt McClain 113tr, / Josh Sisk 20crb, / Tracy A Woodward 154-5; Barry Winiker 111bl; Alex Wong 38-9t.

Courtesy of the International Spy Museum: 140clb, 140bc, 141tr; Mark Finkenstaedt 141b.

iStockphoto.com: benoitb 45cla; davidevison 11cr; dkfielding 4, 55crb; kenex 195tr; kickstand 47bc; Anna Kolesnikova 192bl; kreicher 44bc; miralex 97crb; Sean Pavone 8-9b, 56-7b; Pgiam 16cb, 62-3; RiverNorthPhotography 103br; RomanBabakin 10cl.

Courtesy National Gallery of Art, Washington: 34bl.

Courtesy of National Park Service: Abbie Row 109tr.

National Air and Space Museum, Smithsonian Institution: 8clb, 70-1b, 71tl, 71tr, 73bl; Eric F. Long 20t, 71ftr, 71tc, 72bl, 73tr, 181crb; Dane Penland 73clb, 180, 181clb, 181bl; Carolyn Russo 73crb.

National Gallery Of Art: 21cr, 66-7b, 67cla, Mark Rothko © 1998 Kate Rothko Prizel & Christopher Rothko ARS, NY and DACS, London 2018 Works by Rothko in the, National Gallery's modern art collections 68tl; Alexander Calder © 2018 Calder Foundation, New York/DACS London 2018 Untitled, (1976) 68-9b; Ailsa Mellon Bruce Fund 67tl; Collection of Mr. and Mrs. Paul Mellon 1983.1.24 69clb; Corcoran Collection (Museum Purchase, William A. Clark Fund) 67tr; Samuel H. Kress Collection 1952.2.2 69tr.

National Museum of African American History and Culture: 79clb, 79cb, 79crb, 79fcrb; Alan Karchmer 28-9t, 78clb, 78crb, 78bl, 79t.

National Portrait Gallery, Smithsonian Institution: 93cr.

Newseum: Maria Bryk 94-5b, 95tr; Sam Kittner 95cla.

Rex by Shutterstock: EPA-EFE / Shawn Thew / Amy Sherald First Lady Michelle Obama (2018) - National Portrait Gallery, Smithsonian Institution; gift of Kate Capshaw and Steven, Spielberg; Judith Kern and Kent Whealy; Tommie L. Pegues and Donald A., Capoccia; Clarence, DeLoise, and Brenda Gaines; Jonathan and Nancy Lee Kemper; The Stoneridge Fund of Amy and Marc Meadows; Robert E. Meyerhoff and Rheda, Becker; Catherine and Michael Podell; Mark and Cindy Aron; Lyndon J. Barrois and, Janine Sherman Barrois; The Honorable John and Louise Bryson; Paul and Rose, Carter; Bob and Jane Clark; Lisa R. Davis; Shirley Ross Davis and Family; Alan and, Lois Fern; Conrad and Constance Hipkins; Sharon and John Hoffman;

Audrey M., Irmas; John Legend and Chrissy Teigen; Eileen Harris Norton; Helen Hilton Raiser; Philip and Elizabeth Ryan; Roselyne Chroman Swig; Josef Vascovitz and Lisa, Goodman; Eileen Baird; Dennis and Joyce Black Family Charitable Foundation; Shelley Brazier; Aryn Drake-Lee; Andy and Teri Goodman; Randi Charno Levine and, Jeffrey E. Levine; Fred M. Levin and Nancy Livingston, The Shenson Foundation; Monique Meloche Gallery, Chicago; Arthur Lewis and Hau Nguyen; Sara and John, Schram; Alyssa Taubman and Robert Rothman 93br.

Smithsonian American Art Museum: Ken Rahaim 92-3t; Nam June Paik @ Nam June Paik Estate *Electronic Superhighway: Continental U.S., Alaska, Hawaii* (1995) fifty-one channel video installation (including one closed-circuit, television feed), custom electronics, neon lighting, steel and wood; color, sound Gift of the artist 34-5tc.

Courtesy of the Smithsonian's National Museum of American History: 76cl, 76-7b, 77tl, 77tr, 77cla.

Courtesy of Leo Villareal: James Ewing / Leo Villareal *Multiverse* (2008) -LEDs, custom software & electrical hardware, suspension material Site-specific permanent installations, National Gallery of the Arts Washington, DC 11tr.

Front flap: Alamy Stock Photo: Hunter Bliss cla; Rob Crandall bl; Ian Dagnall t; Sean Pavone cra; Gary Tognoni cb; **Getty Images:** Eric Sturdivant br.

Sheet map cover: Alamy Stock Photo: Zoonar GmbH.

Cover images:
Front and spine: **Alamy Stock Photo:** Zoonar GmbH.
Back: **Alamy Stock Photo:** Sean Pavone cl; Philip Scalia c; Zoonar GmbH; **Getty Images:** Doug Armand tr.

For further information see: www.dkimages.com

Penguin
Random
House

Main Contributers Paul Franklin, Susan Burke, Alice Powers, Jennifer Quasha, Kem Sawyer

Senior Editor Ankita Awasthi Tröger

Senior Designer Owen Bennett

Project Art Editors Dan Bailey, Toby Truphet, Stuti Tiwari Bhatia, Priyanka Thakur

Design Assistant William Robinson

Factchecker Taraneh Jerven

Editors Danielle Watt, Becky Miles

Proofreader Debra Wolter

Indexer Helen Peters

Senior Picture Researcher Ellen Root

Picture Research
Harriet Whitaker, Sumita Khatwani, Mark Thomas

Illustrators Stephen Conlin, Gary Cross, Richard Draper, Chris Orr & Associates, Mel Pickering, Robbie Polley, John Woodcock

Senior Cartographic Editor Casper Morris

Cartography Uma Bhattacharya, Reetu Pandey

Jacket Designers
Maxine Pedliham, Bess Daly

Jacket Picture Research Susie Peachey

Senior DTP Designer Jason Little

DTP Coordinator George Nimmo

Senior Producer Stephanie McConnell

Managing Editor Hollie Teague

Art Director Maxine Pedliham

Publishing Director Georgina Dee

This edition updated by
Hansa Barbra, Taraneh Jerven, Ankita Sharma, Azeem Siddiqui, Lucy Sienkowska, Stuti Tiwari, Debra Wolter

First edition 2000
Published in Great Britain by Dorling Kindersley Limited, 80 Strand, London, WC2R 0RL

Published in the United States by DK Publishing, 1450 Broadway, Suite 801, New York, NY 10018

Copyright © 2000, 2019 Dorling Kindersley Limited
A Penguin Random House Company
19 20 21 22 10 9 8 7 6 5 4 3 2 1

A CIP catalog record for this book is available from the British Library.

A catalog record for this book is available from the Library of Congress.

ISSN: 1542 1554
ISBN: 978 0 2413 6879 4

Printed and bound in China.

www.dk.com

The information in this
DK Eyewitness Travel Guide is checked regularly.

Every effort has been made to ensure that this book is as up-to-date as possible at the time of going to press. Some details, however, such as telephone numbers, opening hours, prices, gallery hanging arrangements and travel information are liable to change. The publishers cannot accept responsibility for any consequences arising from the use of this book, nor for any material on third party websites, and cannot guarantee that any website address in this book will be a suitable source of travel information. We value the views and suggestions of our readers very highly. Please write to: Publisher, DK Eyewitness Travel Guides, Dorling Kindersley, 80 Strand, London, WC2R 0RL, UK, or email: travelguides@dk.com

31901065301816